Please Lord, Send Me!

Perry N. Priest

Please Lord, Send Me!

Perry N. Priest

Printed in the United States of America.

This book is dedicated to Anne.
Life with her is like a dream come true!
Faithful, loving wife, prayer warrior,
full partner in all the different aspects of the work.

What more can I say?
I think I might have quit somewhere along the way
if she hadn't been given to me.

Thanks, Anne!

Forward

For a number of years I have wanted to put some of my father's stories into book form for others to read and enjoy. These stories were never intended to go together. They are Dad's words, but are not necessarily meant to flow from one section to the next. You should be able to read each section as a stand-alone reading, although we *have* tried to put them in a logical but not necessarily chronological order. Some of them are taken from prayer letters, family letters, and others he wrote specifically thinking he would like them published. I tried to choose ones that give an overview of my parents' life. Dad also convinced Mom to add a few articles, so you will see a few written by her.

When my brothers and I were children, a favorite song of my brother Daniel was "This world is not my home, I'm just a passing through." That's been my parents' attitude towards this life. When they finished their work with the Sirionó (in Bolivia) they didn't rest; they felt like God was leading them to another work (with the Jibu in Nigeria) and they didn't complain or resist. They moved on, believing that the best place to be was in God's will. Retirement has been no different. It may be a different phase in life, but they continue to serve the Lord where they are.

I hope that in this book you will see my father's humor and his love for his wife, his family, the Sirionó and Jibu people, and most especially his love for the Lord and desire for all to have a personal relationship with the God he loves.

Lorna A. Priest

My father passed away on December 11, 2009, just days after seeing the first copy of this book. We were happy he was able to see it. He is with his Lord.

Timeline

- 13 August 1930—birth of Perry in Troy, MS
- 20 February 1931—birth of Anne in Columbia, SC
- 1952—Perry and Anne graduate from Columbia Bible College
- Fall 1952—Anne begins nurses training
- 1953—Perry joins Wycliffe Bible Translators
- 7 January 1954—Perry arrives in Mexico for Jungle Camp
- 28 January 1955—Perry arrives in Peru
- 5 May 1955—Perry arrives in Bolivia
- 1 January 1956—Anne arrives in Mexico for Jungle Camp
- 21 April 1956—marriage in Columbia, SC
- May 1956—arrival in Bolivia as a married couple
- 30 October 1956—allocation to the Sirionó
- 20 March 1957—birth of Bob in Cochabamba, Bolivia
- 25 March 1959—birth of Daniel in Riberalta, Bolivia
- 1960/1961—furlough in Norman, OK and Columbia, SC
- 26 February 1961—birth of Lorna in Columbia, SC
- 1961—Perry gets an MA in Missions from Columbia Bible College ("A Survey of Missionary Activity in Bolivia")
- 29 April 1961—return to Bolivia
- 29 October 1964—birth of Joel in Riberalta, Bolivia
- 1966/1967—furlough in Pontotoc, MS
- 1973/1974—furlough in Pontotoc, MS and Columbia, SC
- September 1977—Sirionó New Testament dedication
- November 1985—left Bolivia
- 1986—Perry taught Bible Translation Principles to potential Bible translators at the Wycliffe center in Dallas, TX
- Summer 1986—return to Bolivia to visit and encourage believers in 11 indigenous groups
- 20 May 1987—arrival in Jos, Nigeria
- June 1987—arrival in Serti, Nigeria
- 28 May 1997—death of Perry's mother
- 23 December 1997—Jesus film video and nine boxes of the Jibu New Testaments arrive in Serti
- February 1998—Jibu New Testament dedication
- 28 April 1999—arrival in USA for a new life

Contents

Introduction

I Never Surrendered To Be a Missionary. After more than 44 years serving the Lord as a missionary and Bible translator overseas, how can I say I never surrendered to be a missionary?

When I was about 10 years old, my uncle saw my love for math, and said to me, "Maybe you should become a CPA. They make $15 a day." At that time a teacher's salary was less than $100 a month, and a day laborer might make less than $2 per day. So, for several years, my ambition was to be a CPA.

When I was 15, Jesus came into my life and I realized He wanted to make me more and more like Himself. This began a spiritual journey, which has continued for 64 years.

Shortly after my conversion, I said to myself (the Holy Spirit speaking to me, I'm sure), "Now that I know Jesus and have eternal life, and since there are millions who have never heard of Him, I want to go and tell them." That was my call and it hasn't grown dim during all the ensuing years. The greatest blessing I've ever had, apart from my loving wife, Anne, and family, has been sharing this Gospel with people who likely would never have heard otherwise.

As I visit different churches, I hear people talk of "surrendering to become a pastor," or "surrendering to be a missionary." My dictionary says "surrender" means "to give up, as to an enemy in warfare."[1] It carries with it the idea of reluctance, sacrifice, maybe even kicking and screaming, having to relinquish something precious. Would a man in love be said to "surrender" to marry his beloved? Would a child be said to "surrender" to eat an ice cream cone?

"Surrender" just isn't the right word. *I begged God to allow* me to be a missionary ("Please Lord, Send Me!"), and He did. I'm glad I didn't become a CPA!

---

[1] Funk and Wagnalls New Standard College Dictionary.

Early Years

One of my first memories is of sitting with Mama and Daddy under the pear tree beside our farmhouse in Troy, Mississippi. Both of them were laughing and feeding me bits of ripe pear.

When I was age three, the doctors said I probably wouldn't live. Mama sat under a peach tree, crying, and committed me to God, accepted His will, then told Him if He spared me, she was giving me to Him for full-time Christian service.

In 1945 I was registering for my sophomore year in Pontotoc High School. A teacher came by and said, "We have a new elective this year. It's Bible. You should sign up for it." Well, I wasn't interested in the Bible, but somehow I found myself in the Bible class. And from day one it began to change my life. No seminary professor could have taught Christ in the Old Testament any better than Miss Sara Wright did. The Word began to have meaning to me. A few weeks into the class, I realized "I believe all of this! Jesus has come into my life!" Then, a few weeks farther along, God impressed me with this thought: "Since I now know Jesus, and since there are millions who haven't heard of Him, I should go and tell them." As I see it now, that was my call to missions—not very dramatic or sensational, but Biblical? Yes, it came straight from the Word.

I don't know how Miss Wright knew of my interest in missions, and I don't know how she knew I was thinking about going to Columbia Bible College in South Carolina, but one day, during my senior year, she met me in the hall with a catalog. She said, "Perry I think God may be telling me to give this to you." It was a catalog from Columbia Bible College, which was her alma mater. I thank God for that confirmation that this was where He wanted me to study.

First Day at College

Miss Wright just loved Dr. Robert McQuilkin, the president of Columbia Bible College (CBC). She had told me so much about him and how happy he was going to be that I was there, that I almost expected him to be at the bus station to meet me!

The day I arrived at the college, this old man with baggy pants and a big old raggedy-looking coat came up to me. He didn't introduce himself but somehow I got the idea he was Dr. McQuilkin. This old man said, "Perry, I want you to go to the hospital with me tonight, and we're going to witness." I'd never witnessed to anybody in my life and I was scared to death but I thought, boy, I'd better go if he tells me. I knew all freshmen were to go to the orientation program that night, but if Dr. McQuilkin asks you to go with him, do you refuse? So I agreed. We went to the hospital that night. He had an autoharp, and would go from room to room, and he would play and sing, and he'd talk to people about Jesus. Then he'd ask me to say a few words. Even before that first night was over I learned that he wasn't Dr. McQuilkin. His name was Mr. Prescott, a wonderful old man who was a strong witness for Jesus Christ.

The next morning I was called to the dean's office. Am I the only student that ever got into trouble with Dean Munro the very first day at CBC?

Extroverts Have More Fun

That first year at CBC I was very inhibited, as I felt everyone else was way ahead of me spiritually. It was during this time that I realized that extroverts have a lot more fun than introverts, and extroverts do a lot more witnessing than introverts. I decided I was going to do my best to be an extrovert. I started really exerting myself and pushing myself more.

Mr. Prescott continued to take me under his wing, and I enjoyed it. On Sunday afternoons we'd go up to the park by the State Capitol. He would sit down and start playing his autoharp, and people would gather around. He'd give a little witness and then he'd ask me to say something, and it was then that I began learning how to tell other people about Jesus Christ. I credit that old man with a lot of good things in my life.

I learned much during those years at CBC. I learned a lot about trusting and obeying, surrendering, authentic Christian living, just looking at the lives of the staff and faculty and that of my roommate. Earl Barnes was the wonderful roommate God gave me that first year. He was a great testimony to me. He said, "Don't you think it would be a good idea to study the Bible together every night?" Well, I'd never thought of such a thing, but we did it, and it was a joy to me and helped to ground me in the Word. Later, Roger Hunt and then Winford Hedrick were great roommates. During the four CBC years, I learned that I could have victory in Christ in any and every situation, and that the Holy Spirit could make me more like Jesus.

I heard about sinking my own well. Instead of depending on the spirituality of others and the relationship they had with God, I could have my own relationship with Him, which included morning devotions, attempting to pray throughout the day, fellowship with Jesus Christ, and honoring him in whatever way I could.

God helped me to witness to many of the soldiers on the street during the years that I was at CBC. We got permission from the chaplain at Fort Jackson to start a Bible study in Chapel #10. Those soldiers told other soldiers about the Bible study and I had a good time for one year going out once a week on Tuesday night and teaching the Word of God to soldiers. Some of them really grew in their faith.

I've been thankful over and over again as a Bible translator for the exegetical skills that I learned at CBC. One of my professors was Mr. Frank Sells. Mr. Sells' statement, "All God's commands are His enablings," has encouraged me again and again over the years.

Those were very happy years. In situations where I can either speak or not speak up for Jesus I try to take the extrovert position. I don't know that I'm an extrovert yet, but it's been fun trying.

Love is in the Air

When I was studying at Columbia Bible College, there was a beautiful girl that usually sat two or three rows in front of me (seating was alphabetical in all the classes), so for four years I watched her and admired her, but I never got the nerve to talk to her seriously about anything.

Toward the end of our senior year, I asked her for a date. She was polite and accepted, but why should she pay attention to me? She was the daughter of Dr. McQuilkin, the president of CBC!

I was working as well as studying. Freshman year at a supermarket, sophomore year, a paper route, then a laundry, and lastly as a salesman, so I always seemed to be behind in at least one of my subjects. On our third date we went to her parents' home where she helped me review for a Hebrew Word Study exam. When I got my grade, I decided she was an excellent teacher. Later we found out I got a better grade in that class than she. Good teacher, good student, good partnership!

After graduation, Anne went to nurses training, and I went to University of Oklahoma to study linguistics and Bible translation. I visited her a couple of times in Chicago, then she visited me in Oklahoma. That's when I made a very messed up proposal to her, but she lovingly helped me to redo it.

Later she told me that her father, Dr. McQuilkin, had told her when we started dating, "Now you be nice to Perry." I believe he was on my side.

During her Bible college days, Anne had thought of going to India and starting an orphanage for 100 children. She would have done well at it, but I'm glad that, instead, she became my partner in Bible translation for the Sirionó people of Bolivia and the Jibu people of Nigeria.

Anne's Testimony

As told by Anne

When I was a child, every summer we went to Ben Lippen Conference grounds near Asheville, North Carolina. It was a wonderful time enjoying the beauty of the mountains, glorious sunsets, wandering freely wherever I wanted to go and attending many of the meetings. One day when I was five years old, as I was playing by myself outside the historic Inn, my eight-year-old brother Robertson came by and informed me, "Everyone at this conference has been born again except you." Now I didn't know what "born again" meant but by the way he said it I knew I needed to be "born again." So I said, "Yes, I have." To which he responded, "No, you haven't." And so ensued a big argument. When he left I ran to my mother and asked her if I had been born again. She explained to me what that meant and asked if I would like to be born into God's family. So it was at that time that I invited Jesus into my heart and life.

However, as the years passed, I was not sure of my salvation and wondered many times if I really was saved. Every time there was an invitation given at a meeting I wondered if I should go forward. When I was nine years old we were once again at Ben Lippen. We ate all our meals at the group dining room. After breakfast we always had a short devotional. This particular morning after the devotional we were leaving the dining room and my mother was sitting over to the side talking with a lady. As I passed by I heard something they were talking about that made me think that the woman had the same problem as I did concerning assurance of salvation. So I stopped to listen. My mother had her read John 3:36 "Whoever believes in the Son has eternal life..." My mother asked the lady, "Do you believe?" "Yes, of course." (I was answering in my heart right along with the lady.) "Then what do you have?" asked my mother. "I don't know; I just can't be sure that I'm really saved." "What does the Bible say you have?" They went over this several times and I was right there eagerly awaiting the answer. Then my mother told the lady that if she said that she believed, God said she had eternal life, and if she doubted that she had eternal life then she was calling God a liar, because He said whoever believes has eternal life. I never knew what happened to

that lady, but in that very instant it completely clicked with me:
"Yes, I believe. I don't want to call God a liar. I believe, and He says
I have eternal life." From that moment on I never doubted my sal-
vation because my faith was not in myself but in God's Word.

Every Friday night of each conference at Ben Lippen we had
a missionary rally. Those who felt God calling them to the mission field would go forward and stand on the platform and give
a verse the Lord had used to call them to the field. Veteran missionaries from all over the world spoke and challenged us to reach
those who had never heard the Gospel. At the very end of these
meetings we would all stand in a circle around Houston Hall holding hands and singing, "Where He leads me I will follow." This, of
course, had a mighty impact upon my life. My father always told
us children that the highest calling anyone could have was to be
a missionary. Is it any wonder that from childhood I felt the Lord
would have me go as a missionary?

When I finished high school, the natural place for me to go
was Columbia Bible College since my father was the president
there. Here too, of course, missions was emphasized. My mother
had started Bethel Camp for black children as there was no other
Christian Camp blacks could attend in those days. The summer
before I began college I was helping my mother at Bethel Camp.
I was supposed to lead games. Some of these girls and guys were
big teenagers. They were rowdy, they were not going to be told
what to do, and I was absolutely at a loss to know how to get them
organized into teams. I was angry with them. I was discouraged. I
went back to my room, threw myself on the bed and cried. "Lord,
how can I ever be a missionary if I don't even love people here? I
have no power to influence, I have no love, and I'm helpless." The
Lord seemed to speak to my heart and say, "Of course you don't,
but you have me and all you need can be found in me." What a
comfort that was.

After my freshman year at CBC I went for the summer to work
as a waitress at Keswick Bible Conference in New Jersey. There
was also a ministry to alcoholics at the same facilities. The very
first night I was there they had a meeting for these men, and we
were invited to attend. The speaker handed out verses for different men to read. The first was from Colossians 1:26, 27: "...the
mystery that has been kept hidden for ages and generations, but
is now disclosed to the saints...Christ in you, the hope of glory."
Then another man would stand up and read his verse that told
who Jesus was: God, Love, All powerful, etc. After each verse the
leader would go back to the first man and ask, "And where is He?"

"In me!" On and on the verses went, telling of Christ and His great-ness. After each verse the leader would come back to the first man with the glorious assurance that this very Christ was in me. This had a powerful impact on my life that has stuck with me through-out the years. That fall when I went back to CBC I studied the Epis-tles under Buck Hatch and they came alive to me as I saw that truly, just as I had learned in the summer, this wonderful Christ is in me to work out His good will.

While I was at CBC I decided I'd never marry a Baptist because in my opinion Baptists seemed to think they were the only ones who were right. Nor would I marry someone going with Wycliffe Bible Translators; they were too intellectual and I was not. Then I met and fell in love with Perry and he was both a Baptist and was going to go as a missionary with Wycliffe, so that changed my mind right fast!

However, as I thought about the importance of God's Word in my own life: for salvation, assurance, daily life, comfort in sor-row, strength for temptation, and guidance. I realized that yes, that is what I'd like to be involved in: giving God's Word to those who didn't have it in their own language so that they too could ex-perience God's salvation, comfort, guidance, and strength in their own lives. And that has been our joy down through the years.

Two Angels

The year was 1954. I had finished two summers of linguistic training at University of Oklahoma, been accepted as a Bible translator by Wycliffe Bible Translators (WBT), and then survived (and enjoyed) the three-month Jungle Camp Training in southern Mexico. I was ready to go to the foreign field, but had no money and no promised support. (Wycliffe does not provide salaries for its missionaries but expects each one to trust the Lord to provide for all his or her needs through God's people.) WBT informed me that I was free to proceed to the field when I had at least three months' support in hand or promised.

Since I didn't know how or where to "raise support," I went to Memphis, Tennessee and worked for Sears five days a week and sold Bibles on Saturdays. One afternoon as I picked up my mail at the rooming house, I noticed a note on the back of one of the letters. It said, "Please call Norris Griffin," then a telephone number. I had no idea who this person was, and I was surprised that someone would look at my mail and write on it.

I called, and the man said, "I want to invite you to a monthly missionary prayer meeting on Poplar Street." We chatted, and I accepted the invitation. Then I asked him how he had known I was a Christian. He said, "I'm your mailman, and all your letters are from Wycliffe or from Columbia Bible College." Norris became my friend, and a great encourager. He also was concerned not only that I'd have enough money to get to the field, but also enough promised support to stay long term. He was directly or indirectly responsible for many members of the prayer group and also for three Memphis churches becoming long-term supporters of our work. Norris never became a foreign missionary, but I consider him to have had a big part in our work over the years. God sent him to me at just the time I needed an encourager and advocate.

Also in that prayer group was a nurse, Mary Spence. A few years later, Mary asked us for permission to print and mail out our prayer letters. We gladly turned the job over to her. She faithfully saw that each letter was printed, two hundred or more envelopes addressed and stuffed, and the letters mailed out several times a year for almost four decades. She also kept up with all the address changes, a huge job in this mobile society. Recently she wrote us to say, "Helping you with the prayer letter has been one of the greatest joys of my life!"

Norris and Mary are two of our heroes, angels sent by God to help reach the unreached with the Word in a language they can understand.

Uncle Cam

William Cameron Townsend, founder of Wycliffe Bible Translators, was best known by most of us as "Uncle Cam." My impression of him, even before I joined Wycliffe in 1953, was that he was
a man of great faith in a great God.

One special memory I have of Uncle Cam happened in 1954. I
had already finished my formal Bible training in South Carolina
and my linguistic training at University of Oklahoma, and was almost ready to leave for the field. Anne was still in nurses training and wouldn't be able to leave for the field for another sixteen
months. We were engaged, but secretly, as the board had ruled
that members could not become engaged to non-members.

Our plan was that I would go on to the field, and when Anne became a member, we'd announce our engagement. Then she would
join me and we'd be married in South America. I began to feel that
I should let the WBT board know of our engagement. So I wrote
them, along with a copy to Uncle Cam. I got quick answers from
both. I received no congratulations from the board. They said I
couldn't proceed to South America, as I was engaged to a non-
member. After a few days of brooding over their decision, I received a letter from Uncle Cam. He congratulated me on the engagement, and he said it was wonderful that I had found a wife
who wanted to serve the Lord with me. He said he knew Anne's
family well, and was sure she would make an excellent wife and
Bible translator. And then the best news of all: I should proceed to
the field as soon as possible. It was not difficult for me to make the
decision to obey Uncle Cam rather than the board. So I went on to
Peru, where I was welcomed by Uncle Cam and other missionaries. Uncle Cam taught me how to relate to government officials,
university professors, indigenous people, and others. He taught
me how to include government officials in areas of the work in
which there was a mutual interest, such as literacy, medical work,
bilingual schools, and community development.

Uncle Cam and his wife, Elaine, taught Anne and me that one
of the easiest and best ways to witness for Christ to government
officials is to relate incidents about how the indigenous people
respond to the Word as it becomes available to them in their own
language. I've related similar testimonies dozens of times, usually

quoting Scriptures such as Psalm 119:130, "The unfolding of your words gives light..." I've never seen any criticism or lack of interest in such testimonies on the part of government officials.

Perry and Anne

Starting Tumi Chucua

In 1955 I went to Lima, Peru to study Spanish. I expected to translate the Bible for an indigenous language group in either Brazil or Peru. After a few months of language study I flew to the mission headquarters in Peru.

The mountains we flew over were beautiful. It was a very clear day, and we could see below us the high rugged peaks, many of them capped with snow, and the beautiful mountain valleys between, with an occasional house or village. I wondered how many of those mountain people had ever heard of the grace of Jesus.

Soon after my arrival at the center in Peru I began hearing that our mission director, Uncle Cam Townsend, had signed an agreement with the president of Bolivia to begin a ministry of Bible translation, linguistic investigation, and other helps to the various indigenous communities in Bolivia. Uncle Cam asked me to go, along with Cal Hibbard, to make the initial survey in Bolivia, confirm the agreement with the government, find possible sites for a center of operations, and find out as much as possible where translations were needed.

Cal and I saw the Lord's hand in every tiny detail. We were given a royal welcome by the cabinet member under whom we were to work. Then he sent us to a department under him. The head of that department was exceptionally cordial, and assigned two of his men to stay right with us the two weeks we were in La Paz to help with government letters, requests, and anything else we needed.

We also had a short appointment with the vice-president of Bolivia. He didn't say many words, but what he did say was very wonderful: "The country of Bolivia is very pleased and grateful that you have the desire to help the indigenous people of Bolivia. It is so refreshing to come in contact with those who are interested in helping others. Nowadays everyone is interested only in bettering himself, and in egotistical ends, and the spirit of sacrifice is lacking. We are so glad to welcome you who come with the apostolic spirit, and with the willingness to live and serve among the lowland language groups." Then he assured us of the government's help in every way possible.

After our time in La Paz we flew to Riberalta. Riberalta was a little lowland town of about ten thousand people. At that time there were a couple of trucks and about ten jeeps there, all brought up the Amazon River by boat. The trucks were used to haul Brazil nuts and other cargo to and from the airport. A few days after we arrived, our Bolivia field director Harold Key and our pilot Ralph Borthwick, arrived from Peru in a small float plane. They picked out a spot for the center—a beautiful lake about two miles long with an island in the middle, and about a half mile from the Beni river. We anticipated the river would be our main source of supplies. The lake was about 15 miles up river from Riberalta. As a single man I lived at the site on the lake with 13 soldiers and 21 Bolivian workers to clear out a place along the lake for the first houses (it was dense forest). We partially lived off the land. One morning one of the men cut a bee-tree, so we had some honey, then one night another of the fellows brought in the heart of a certain type of palm tree, which was very good. I ate so much monkey and alligator meat during that time that I never wanted to see it again.

Six new missionary families joined us a few weeks later. We had put up several temporary roofs and one long house for everyone to live in. Each family had one room until we were able to build homes for individual families.

This beautiful center on the lake came to be called Tumi Chucua (a Tacana word meaning "Island of Palms") and was our mission's center of operations for most of the 30 years we were in Bolivia.

One of my jobs was to visit and survey several language groups where we would allocate translation teams (two single ladies or a family in each place).

Gradually Tumi Chucua began to grow. Missionaries who were skilled in jobs such as pilots, mechanics, radio technicians, medical workers, and MK (missionary kid) teachers were crucial to the work.

Bolivians in the local area were hired for various jobs. Some built houses for themselves and their families, not far from the mission houses. Our fellow missionary, Dave Farah, supervised these workers. He had a gift for leading the workers and our neighbors to Christ, so a Spanish-speaking church was soon begun. Over the years, that church has birthed half a dozen other churches, and several of the workers and their sons became pastors.

Our translators spent most of their time in their indigenous locations, but they came to Tumi Chucua for annual conference, medical needs, and translation workshops.

Tumi Chucua was our home away from home for most of our thirty years in Bolivia.

The Telegram

In 1955 and 1956 I did a lot of survey work in Bolivia to help determine which indigenous language groups were most in need of Scriptures in their own language. Since I was single, and a "more experienced missionary" (by weeks or months only), I was appointed to accompany new translators to their first language assignments.

Anne had gotten an unheard-of permission from nursing school to take the three-month linguistics courses at the University of Oklahoma in the summer of 1955. She would apply to Wycliffe at that time as well, and receive her letter of acceptance (or possibly rejection because of a heart murmur) in August. She was to send me the results via telegram.

Well, the telegram came the evening before I was to accompany Gil and Marian Prost to their first assignment to the Chacobo people. I was to be with them for a month. There would be no mail service. The telegram said only, "Ouch love Anne." What did it mean? There was no way to find out.

The Prosts and I proceeded to the isolated village location, and for the whole month all I could think of was "Ouch love Anne." Was she accepted into Wycliffe Bible Translators, or not? What would we do if she were not? That may have been the hardest month of my life. You see, I was in love.

When I returned to Tumi Chucua (our mission center of operations), I was overjoyed to find a letter from Anne awaiting me, saying that the telegram should have said, "Accepted, much love, Anne."

Now if you know the Morse code, you'll realize there's just a slight difference in the letter "o" and the letter "m". "M" is two dashes and "o" is three dashes. Just that little difference between ouch and much.

We figured the telegraph operator assumed that "Accepted" referred to the message having been received, so he just omitted that key word when typing the telegram.

I've always loved puzzles, but not that one.

At Home with the Sirionó

After Anne and I married, we were assigned to live and work with the Sirionó people. We first lived in San Pedro, Bolivia where about 70 Sirionó lived. We learned to speak the language, formulated a scientific alphabet, began work on the translation of the Bible, and began literacy classes.

Would you like to come with us for a visit to the home of some of our Sirionó friends? You'll have to have good balance to keep from falling off the log that leads through the deep mud to the door of their house. It's rainy season, and with the children, pigs, and dogs playing around the door, the dirt is soon stirred into a mud hole. As we enter the large room we see there is a lack of furniture. There are a few hammocks, a fire in one corner, and baskets containing their few belongings hanging from the wall. However, there would be little room for more, as it is crowded with the four or five families that live here with their chickens and dogs and the occasional pig or goat that wanders in.

The old man in the corner, fixing his arrows, is Hehe. When the Sirionó lived, as nomads, in the forest he was chief of one group. His word is still respected. His two wives sit around cooking yuca in the fire and talking to the other women. One nurses a thin, sickly boy of a year and a half. She is blind in one eye and certainly would win no beauty contest. She is a great talker and likes to joke. Hehe raised his other wife from childhood. She is quieter and very thin and sickly. Several of the men lie around in hammocks resting. Some of the women are mending clothes, others are grating yuca to make coarse flour. The little children crawl around on the dirt floor and the older ones sit around the fire roasting palm nuts or looking for lice in their mothers' hair. I doubt if anyone will invite you to sit down, but they will be happy to talk and laugh with you. If you don't feel like standing, look for a stump to sit on. They'll be happy to tell you about their latest hunt, teach you a word or two in Sirionó, or ask a dozen questions about your family. As you leave, they'll all shout, "Come back soon," and you'll know that you have made several new and interesting friends.

Housing and Privacy

When we went to live with the Sirionó people we didn't want to seem too affluent (not that we were), so we built a Sirionó-style house—poles, leaf roof, dirt floor, mud walls. Their doorways had no doors, but I did make and put up a screen door for our house to keep out chickens, dogs, and pigs.

The people felt free to come into the house at any time during the day whether we were studying, cooking, or resting! We did try, without much success, to get them to call or knock when they came at night. *But* calling or knocking just wasn't in their culture. Coughing, grunting, or clearing the throat were acceptable ways to get one's attention, and lots of that went on regularly at our door as people came each time they needed Nurse Ana to help with everything from delivering babies to treating stomach aches. One man apparently had no success getting our attention, so he came right into the bedroom in the middle of the night. Imagine Anne's fright as she woke up from a sound sleep to see this big man hovering over her, coughing and clearing his throat. The next day Anne insisted I put a hook on the door so it could be secured at night.

After that, the people began to come to the bedroom window, not much farther from us than the big man had been, to do their coughing and throat clearing. This time, I planted a garden of okra and tomatoes under the window and made a pole fence around it, and no gate! Gotta stay ahead of 'em some way!

Hehe

Army Ants

Long lines of big, fast-moving army ants can often be seen in the Amazon. Sometimes they invade homes, especially at night. The Sirionó call them "hunters."

One night, shortly after midnight, Anne and I realized that our mosquito net, bed, floor, and walls were covered with ants. Some had found a way to slip under the net and enter the bed. One large column of ants was moving up and across our mosquito net and the crib where baby Bob was sleeping. Other columns were on the packed earthen floor and on the mud walls. On the floor were many cockroaches and other insects, chased from their hiding places and being devoured by the ants.

As new missionaries we had no idea how to combat the ants. I got out of bed, stood in a basin of water, and kept wadding up papers, setting them afire and throwing them at the ants all over the floor.

We had just received a bundle of Saturday Evening Post magazines. We were sorry to have to burn them, especially the jokes and cartoons, as English reading matter was scarce. So Anne, standing in another basin of water (with baby in arms), would read the jokes to me, before tearing the page out to give to me to burn.

After an hour or so we won the battle—the ants left us. Later, as we told the story to neighbors, they laughed and informed us we could have chased the ants away fast just by sprinkling water all over the floor. After that, we had many other invasions of "hunter" ants, and found that the water method works best. And playing with water at midnight is a lot less dangerous than playing with fire.

We didn't mind losing the hour or two of sleep, but we did grieve over having to burn all those new-to-us English magazines.

No Room

Traditionally, the Sirionó religion consisted mainly of worship of the moon as creator, extreme fear and appeasement of evil spirits, and prayer to the bones of departed warriors and hunters.

Echobe was the man who helped us most in those early years, first to learn the language and then to begin translation of the Scriptures. He and his wife Petrona were the first to show evidence of really coming to faith in Christ and allowing Him to be Lord of their lives.

One day he said something like this to me: "You know how afraid our people are of the spirits. We don't go to the forest alone, and we don't like to be alone at night, as the evil spirits talk to us and bother us and frighten us. But since Christ has come into my life, the spirits haven't bothered me even once, and I'm no longer afraid."

Some time later, we were at our headquarters at Tumi Chucua when the Bolivian Air Force told us they were sending some of their officers to Tumi Chucua for a two-day vacation. There would be eighteen men. Protocol told us we could sleep two to each room, except that the general should have a room by himself. That meant they would need ten rooms. Well, we moved some of the missionary kids together, and we were able to find nine rooms for them. But where could we put the extra person? No more rooms were available. We decided protocol would have to take a back seat to convenience, and the general would have to be put in a room with another officer.

The first night, I as field director, invited the general and his assistants to eat supper with us. During the meal Anne and I usually try to share with visitors something of our Christian beliefs and motivation and relationship with the indigenous people. That night I happened to tell of Echobe's lack of fear of the evil spirits now that he knows Christ.

The general then said, "I think I need what that man has. I've always been afraid even to sleep in a room by myself. I always feel better if someone is there with me."

When he said that, both Anne and I smiled inwardly. The Lord must have known all along that we needed nine rooms instead of ten.

The Man in the Basket

Long ago, when the Sirionó people were still nomadic, they would leave their dead relatives on a platform in the forest. Months later, when their journey brought them back to the place where they had left a corpse, they would try to find the bones of the departed one, especially the skull and, if he was a good hunter, the arm bones. The presence of the arm bones was thought to give extra strength and accuracy in using the bow and arrows, on which they depended for their livelihood. The bones were put in a basket woven of palm leaves. The basket of bones would be carried with them, sometimes for years, in their wanderings. The belief was that prayer to the bones of the person could bring results, especially in finding and killing game.

When the nights were cool, the basket of bones would be placed near the fire so the person wouldn't suffer the cold. This custom had been lost and replaced by burial (in the ground) before Anne and I began work among the Sirionó.

I did, however, have one experience with a basket of bones. New Tribes Mission was beginning a work with the Yuquí language group (distant cousins of the Sirionó), and they asked me to visit them and help evaluate the similarities and differences in the two languages.

While I was there, I found that I could understand parts of their language, and they could understand parts of what I said in Sirionó. But we all agreed the languages were too different, which meant that the Yuquí would need a separate translation of the Scriptures in their own language.

One day as I visited a Yuquí camp, the people invited me to spend the night with them. I countered, "I don't have a hammock." (They all slept in hammocks—no beds.) One young man said, "You can use mine. I'll sleep on the ground." So I agreed. That night I got up in the dark, and stumbled over a basket. The whole group of several families began to shout and were very agitated. I thought they sounded very angry with me. I had stepped on and violated the bones of one of their great hunters[1]. As the angry shouting continued, I thought I was in real trouble. Finally

---

[1] Later I learned that the bones were the remains of the old chief's son, who had been a great hunter. He was killed with a shotgun when the

the shouting stopped. The chief saw that I was concerned—maybe more for myself than for the bones—and he assured me that nobody was angry with me. Anytime the bones were disturbed the shouting was done, he explained, to keep the evil spirits away. Even so, I was careful not to again disturb "the man in the basket."

Yuquí tried to raid a settlement of farmers in order to get metal tools (such as axes, knives and shovels).

Old Pablo

*Pablo died Saturday, June 22, 1963. The following is
an account of the events just prior to,
and on the day of, his death.*

Old Pablo died this morning. He had been very sick with tuberculosis for several months. He felt that he was going up to see Jesus when he died. His face was always one of the brightest with interest when listening to the stories of Jesus in our Sunday night gatherings. A week or so ago he told me that he dreamed the people had told him to return (meaning that the spirits of the departed dead had told him not to die yet). This is a very common dream among sick people, and they expect to recover if they have this dream. Another time he dreamed that he told Jesus, "I'm very mean," and Jesus had just answered, "I love you." About two days before his death he said that Jesus was tugging at his legs. This parallels another very common dream: people who are very sick often dream that the people who have gone before are pulling them into the next world. This dream commonly precedes death by a few days or weeks, and the sick person loses all hope of recovery after experiencing this type of dream.

At approximately 9:30 a.m. we were told that Pablo was dead. We went over and ducked through the door into the crowded little house. Pablo lay in his small hammock made of *ambaibo* bark. He was still breathing but he was unable to move or talk. Several women sat or squatted around him. Some were softly wailing, especially his wife Maria and his 'sister' Eromii ('One Leaf'). Eromii is actually his parallel cousin, but parallel cousins are as closely related in the Sirionó way of reckoning relationships as are brothers and sisters. In fact, one Sirionó term includes all three of these relationships. Several men were standing inside, silently watching.

While we were there several people came in, one or two at a time, and several left, one or two at a time. There was very little talking—only a short sentence every once in a while.

Presently the women took Pablo out of the hammock and placed him on a palm-leaf mat on the ground (this procedure also is according to custom). Several children quietly sat, played, and platted hair in the house, sometimes stepping across the dying man.

Pablo was wearing trousers and shirt which had been patched so much that very little of the original material was still in evidence. Just after placing him on the ground, the women put a better pair of trousers on him. They were put on over the ragged trousers, and without any effort to keep the legs of the ragged trousers from sliding up his thin, skinny legs (since the man was very thin and his legs were small, the legs of the original trousers went practically up to the stride). Another patched-up shirt was put on over the original one, and when the second arm was being put into the shirt sleeve, the sleeve tore badly.

When we left a short time later, the man was still breathing. A half hour or so later we knew from the loud wailing that death had at last arrived.

Our son Bob had been over to Pablo's house, and came back with the jaw bone and teeth of a piraña fish. Piraña teeth are very sharp, and are used by the Sirionó to split feathers for putting on arrows. Bob said that Maria was giving away Pablo's possessions, and her gift to him had been the piraña teeth.

Eromii's husband and another man, Salustiano, came back at around 3:30 p.m. from the edge of the forest where they had dug a shallow grave. (The Sirionó used to put their dead up on a stand in the forest and cover them with leaves, but now have accepted the Bolivian custom of burying.) Salustiano announced that they were now going to take Pablo out, so we went over to watch and help. Two small mats were placed in the center of the house, on which Maria put several dirty rags, none as big as a handkerchief. Then the men placed the corpse on the mats. Two other mats were placed on top of the corpse. The corpse and mats were tied to a bamboo pole with a cord, or small rope, that Maria had originally made for a bow-string. The cord was put around the corpse at the knees and at the neck. Then the two men carried it out, placing the pole on their shoulders. Eromii remarked that it should be tied around the waist, too, as the body was sagging and looked like it would slip out and fall. The men paid no attention to her.

They took the body directly to the grave, and several men, women, and children followed. The body was lowered at once into the grave and covered by the same two men. The wife and sister cried while the grave was being covered.

Ordinarily, as soon as the grave is covered, the people all return home. Today, however, since Pablo had expressed a love for the Savior, I called the attention of those present to Jesus, the only one who can give life, and then led in a short prayer, praying for the wife and the other Sirionó there. Then we all returned home.

Ari and Yande

Ari lay dying in her hammock, her face sooty from weeks of lying by her fire. No one cared enough to warm water to wash her face. She cried out in fear, "People, look at me! The enemy, the enemy!" Later she told her daughter, "I'm going now," and crawled out of her hammock to die on the damp mud floor. Ari had nearly died before but had gotten better for a short time. During that time we had been able to explain the Gospel to her. She was interested, thought heaven must be pretty, knew her heart was dirty with sin, but the fact of Christ's death for her sin didn't seem to enter into her understanding. As far as we know she died without Christ. No one seemed to care particularly when she died. We joined the few Sirionó who went to the burial. To get there we had to go through heavy underbrush, thick with mosquitoes. They laid her in the shallow grave with her hammock beside her. Also, according to Sirionó custom, they left her drinking vessel and eating utensils by her grave to be used in the next life. Though it was a sad little gathering from a physical point of view, how much sadder it was to realize one had gone into eternity without Christ.

Yande's death was different. He, too, had lived for many years in fear of death, and had awakened many times in a cold sweat after dreaming that "the spirits" were pulling at him.

The spirits had not bothered Yande of late. "I know Jesus now; the spirits don't bother those who know Jesus," was his explanation.

But Yande knew that "to be absent from the body is to be present with the Lord," and was no longer afraid of death, which came one day while we were away. Yande knew death was near, and his attitude was one that the unbelievers, and even some of the believers, couldn't comprehend. "I'm happy now; I'm going to heaven now," he said as he lay down and died. The body was wrapped in a reed mat and buried in a shallow grave. The believers stood by the grave and sang some of his favorite songs, then two of them led in prayer. This was the first Sirionó-only Christian funeral among the Sirionó of the Rio Blanco.

Funerals and Arrows

Shortly after we moved to Ibiato, another Sirionó village, one of the important hunters died. We gathered at the cemetery for a short burial service. Then we went out to a clearing in the forest and the men began to shoot their long arrows into the air. They seemed to be enjoying it, and one of them gave me his bow and arrows and told me to try it. I couldn't shoot as high as they could, but they appreciated my efforts.

When we got home, Anne asked me, "Do you know what you just did?" "Sure," I said, "I tried to shoot arrows as high as they did."

"You were helping them chase the evil spirits away from the dead man," she reminded me. Yes, I knew that they customarily shot arrows to chase the spirits away to protect themselves and the deceased. But I had completely forgotten it. So I guess I did help.

It worked. Nobody reported the presence of evil spirits for several days after that.

The Feud Between the Tiger and the Moon

A long time ago the moon, who was a very good wild pig hunter, lived on the earth. One day when he came home from the hunt, he found that his sons had been eaten. He was very angry. "Did you eat my sons?" he asked the animals. "No," they all said. He asked the porcupine. "No, I didn't eat them," the porcupine said. But the moon was so angry he twisted the porcupine's tail, and that is why the porcupine has a twisted tail. "Did you eat my sons?" he asked the funny-faced blackbird. "No," said the blackbird. But the moon was so mad he threw the blackbird against the tree and that is why he has such a flat face. "Did you eat my sons?" he said to the big turtle. "No," said the big turtle. The moon was so angry he kept stepping on the big turtle, and that's why the turtle's shell has cracks all over it. "Did you eat my sons?" he asked the terrapin. "No," said the terrapin. But the moon was so angry he kept stepping on the terrapin, and that is why the terrapin's stomach is concave now. He also threw the monkeys up in the trees and that is where they live now. He went everywhere saying, "Where is the eater of my sons?" and asking everyone, "Who ate my sons?" and the animals said, "We don't know."

It was really the tigers, and the animals had put baskets over the tigers to hide them, so the moon didn't see them.

One day the tigers started across the bamboo pole across the river, and the moon was on the other side. He said, "Come on over." The male tiger started first and when he got halfway across, the moon quickly twisted the bamboo. The tiger fell in the water and the piraña fish ate him. The female, who was pregnant, ran into the forest, and pretty soon gave birth. Tigers have been giving birth ever since, and that is why there are so many tigers.

The female tiger almost started across first, and if she had, then she would have been eaten and there would have been no more tigers.

If the tigers hadn't eaten the moon's sons, the moon would still be with us. But he became angry and said, "I'm going away forever," and spliced bamboo together and climbed up to the sky, where he has lived ever since that day. He is our father.

Creative Writing

Part of our job among the Sirionó people was to give them an alphabet that represented all the sounds of the language. Then there was the literacy program—teaching them to read and write their language. We started a creative writing course. Here are some of their creations, translated into English.

Our Airplane Trip

When one flies up through the sky, it causes his heart to go *cuã cuã cuã* very fast. The airplane jumps around, one's ears stop up, and the worst thing is that one doesn't know if he will come down in a good way. The one who causes the plane to fly is the only one who really enjoys it.

At first we could look down and see cattle, houses, and the river. Then we couldn't see anything but forest.

My son, trembling, said, "I'll never again get in an airplane. One could get lost forever up here. And what if we fall?"

I told him not to think like that, but just to trust our Heavenly Father.

By Edy Ino

The Hard Life

Our people used to live in the forest. Their houses were just upright palm leaves in a circle. They didn't wear clothes. They didn't have mosquito nets. They didn't have anything to cover themselves with at night. They slept in bark hammocks with small fires around them. They did have bows and arrows. They also had stone axes for cutting down trees to get wild honey.

We were constantly at war with the enemy people. They killed many of us. They would kill the men, bash the babies against trees, and capture the women. They say the enemy people stank so badly one could hardly stand it.

The enemy would come early in the morning while the people were still sleeping. Yelling, they would enter the house, killing the people. After stacking up the bodies in the house, they would burn it to the ground.

Life used to be pretty bad.

By Hernan Eato

How the Vulture Finds its Food

The people were all very hungry. "Why don't we go look for *ndia* fruit?" someone said.

"Let's go. What else is there to eat?" they said.

"You climb the tree," they said to one old man. When he reached a fork in the tree, he sat down and began eating the fruit greedily.

"Throw some down to us," the people said. But he just kept eating. The people became so enraged that someone took a green fruit and threw it angrily against the tree. The tree suddenly grew to be very big and tall, and the old man couldn't get down. Everyone else went home, and he was left up in the tree.

During the night, he caught and killed many of the bats that were flying around. He stretched them out on the big branches. Finally wasps came to get bites of meat.

"Go get the vultures; I'll feed them," the old man said.

The wasps flew off and told the vultures. They all came—the common vulture, the big black vulture, and others. The white vulture, which is the leader of all vultures, sat down beside the man and they talked.

"If you will get me down, I'll give you all of this meat," he said, "and I'll always show you meat for your food."

The white vulture agreed and all of the vultures took hold of the man—his arms, fingers, hair, ears, legs, and all of his body. Others flew under him to hold him up. Together they took him safely down to the ground.

The man kept his promise and his spirit still shows the vultures where to find their food. He shows the food to the wasps and the wasps tell the vultures where it is. The vultures don't have any trouble finding food now.

By Nataniel Jacinto

Respecting God's Word

One time God whipped me. It was after I had heard His Word. Even after hearing the Word, I got drunk.

That night as I staggered along the path, a rattlesnake bit me. I bled all over; even my gums and mouth bled. I was given medicine and got well, even though I was almost dead.

That incident has made me think deeply; now I want to be more respectful of God and His Word.

By Vicente Ino

Old Man 'Fraidy Cat

One time an old man and his wife went out to get firewood. Along the way they saw tiger tracks.

"Look at this! An evil beast is around here!" the man said, trembling with fear and climbing up a tree.

"Why are you climbing the tree?" the old woman asked.

"Because of the tiger."

"You can stay up there if you want to, but I'm going on," the wife said.

When the old woman got back to camp, everyone asked where her husband was.

"I left him."

"Why?" they asked.

"Because he's afraid of a tiger's footprint," she said.

So from then on the man's name became "Old Man 'Fraidy Cat."

Story & picture by Echosoi

Sirionó Social Security

Historically, the Sirionó were nomadic forest dwellers. The problem of obtaining enough food, especially meat, is an ever-present one. Every Sirionó has many times experienced the pangs of hunger, and fear of hunger is the motivation and passion that traditionally ruled their thoughts and lives. There is no greater joy to the Sirionó than to have a few days' supply of meat. The depression and unhappiness of the people when no meat is available make conversation with them all but impossible.

My own observations and field notes parallel those of anthropologist Allen Holmberg. Holmberg illustrates again and again how this preoccupation with the quest for food influences every phase of Sirionó life. He states, "Data were recorded on seventy-five disputes that came to my attention...It is significant to note that forty-four of them arose directly over questions of food... Here we have overwhelming evidence of the important role played by food in Sirionó society. It is the most prominent cause of in-group strife."[1]

Most Sirionó dreams are related directly to the eating of food, the hunting of game, and the collecting of edible products from the forest.

The scarcity of and preoccupation with food, the extreme stinginess of the people, and the abandonment of those who are too old or sick to provide for themselves would, except for one factor, ensure the immediate death of the aged. That many do continue to live after their usefulness has passed is due almost entirely to the Sirionó system of food taboos, which do not apply, or apply only very loosely, to the aged. Therefore the aged, even in a society not particularly concerned with their welfare, are assured of certain foods that cannot be eaten by others.

There are hundreds of food taboos, but an arbitrary listing of only a few dozen will give the reader an idea of how the Sirionó unwittingly help to protect their aged against starvation.

---

[1] Holmberg, Allan R. 1969. *Nomads of the Long Bow: The Siriono of Eastern Bolivia.* Garden City, New York: The Natural History Press. Published for The American Museum of Natural History. p 154.

The following list is a free translation of statements by various informants.

- If you eat the young of spider monkey, howler monkey, or yellow monkey, your lips will turn white (anemic).
- If you eat the young of the big hawk, you will become very heavy.
- If you eat the young of agouti or squirrel, your jaw will swell (infected tooth, toothache).
- If you eat fish heads, you will suffer from nosebleed.
- If you eat animal heads (especially brains), your hair will turn gray early. (An example of their evidence is that Hehe, a great hunter, who has never eaten brains, still has black hair even though several men younger than he are already gray.)
- If you eat the heads of ducks and cranes, your children will have long necks.
- If you eat the fat of the land turtle, you will be slow like the land turtle.
- If you eat turtle liver, you will shoot animals in the liver. (Instead of in the more vital heart area.)
- If you eat the small anteater, you will become disobedient.
- If you eat anything that you yourself shoot, your running will be impaired. (Good runners are the best hunters.)
- If you eat corn at night, your teeth will decay. (The explanation is that at night one can't see the worms and weevils, which are bad for the teeth.)
- If you eat meat at night, your armpits will smell. (The tiger can smell you better and follow you.)
- If you eat the small turtle your neck will swell (goiter).
- Men and boys must give manioc and sweet potatoes that are damaged (when being dug from the ground) to the old people.
- Children must give their game and fish to the old people. The children will get sick if they don't do this.
- Young women must not eat palm cabbage that they themselves have chopped out of the palm tree.
- You should not use new gourd drinking-vessels. If you do, you will be sick. You should let the old people use them until they are no longer new, then you can use them.
- If you eat the feet of animals, you will fall frequently.
- If you eat hip blades, your hip blades will become sore.

- If a man or his wife eats breasts of female animals, the wife's breast will harden.
- You should not eat the intestines or stomach of large animals such as deer and tapir. If you do, you will have stomachache and diarrhea and have to stop when you are chasing an animal.
- Only women and old people eat palm heart that grows near the *ahai* tree. (The *ahai* tree is used in puberty rites for girls.)
- If you eat bagre-fish (*mbarae*), your liver will be perforated. (Some even say your children's livers will be affected.)
- If you eat electric eel, your children's legs will not be sturdy and their necks will swell (goiter).
- If you eat surubi-fish (catfish), your children will have big mouths.
- If you eat pacu-fish, your children will be striped.
- If you eat an ear of corn from which rats have eaten, your teeth will hurt.
- If you eat fruit from a tree that has fallen of itself, the spirit that made the tree fall will make you sick.
- If you eat striped agouti, your babies' hair will fall out.
- When a person kills his first tapir or tiger, he should give away his eating utensils and drinking vessels.
- When a person kills his first tapir or tiger, he must not eat any boiled meat or honey for several days. (Yande's uncle broke this taboo and died a few days later.)
- If boys eat squirrel, they will never be good tapir hunters.
- If you eat the male howler monkey, you will have bad dreams and yell at night.
- The eating of any soft meat (the very young offspring, including unborn offspring) is likely to cause toothache.

Most results of breaking taboos (such as not being able to find game, hair turning gray, being lazy) would not disturb the older people much, since they are already old and less active anyway. Since many consequences of taboo-breaking affect the offspring of the guilty person, the women are free to ignore the taboos at an earlier age than are the men.

The penalties for breaking certain taboos are much more severe than those for breaking others.

Certain taboos are therefore adhered to much more rigidly than others.

As it works out, however, the system of taboos, more than anything else, protects the welfare of old people among the Sirionó.

Certain of these taboos are losing their importance now that the Sirionó live with, or in close proximity to, Spanish-speaking people, raise domestic animals, and do some farming. The Gospel has also made them more loving and aware of the needs of the elderly.

Sirionó man with bow and arrows

Health

Anne did a lot of medical work when we lived in San Pedro. Some days she'd work 8-10 hours taking care of the sick. People would come by canoe from as far as three days away from up and down the river because there were no other medical facilities in the area. She was very busy all the time with medical work.

One time we had an epidemic of dysentery in the area. She always kept a lot of medicine, but with this epidemic and so many people who came, she ran out of any medicine for dysentery. After she ran out, our little son Daniel got a really bad case of dysentery. We didn't know what to do about it. Anne had always told the Sirionó, "Here is the treatment you are to take and even when you get better, you're supposed to take all of it; finish the treatment." Well, fortunately a couple of ladies didn't do that, and when they heard that Daniel was sick and that we didn't have medicine they came in their canoe from downriver and said "Here's the medicine we had left over. Will it do you any good?" That was one time Anne didn't fuss at them for not taking all the medicine. The pills were enough to heal Daniel.

Another time, on a Saturday, Anne and I were sorting through medicines. She would get medicines by the barrel full (physician's samples). A lot of it wasn't useful for Bolivia. After it got a little bit old we'd go through it all and decide what to keep and what to throw away. We would fill up the wastebasket, and I'd take it out and pour it down the hole in the outhouse and then fill up another wastebasket. Late that Saturday night, somehow we left some medicine in the wastebasket. Sometime the next day our three-year-old daughter Lorna got hold of it when we were next door. She had taken several medicines, but there was no way to know what she had taken. She began to act crazy, reaching into the air with her hands as though she was grabbing for something, like spider webs. She was seriously ill, and we did what little we could for her, but Anne said it was too late to do very much except just pray that the Lord would spare her life. That was a hard few hours. Finally she was over it.

At another time, our son Joel, who was about 2½ years old, had a strangulated hernia and it came on him very suddenly about the middle of the afternoon. During the time of the peristalsis (when the muscles of the alimentary tract start contracting to move the food and waste on down) he would cry out in terrible pain. That came every 12-15 minutes or so and lasted 3-4 minutes. It seemed like he would die, then it would gradually ease up for a few minutes, and then the terrible pain would come again. We got on the radio and talked to Dr. Neva—our mission doctor—and she told us one or two little things we could try. But there really wasn't much we could do until we got him to a surgeon. It was too late in the day for the airplane to come, but she said, "I'll be on the plane as soon as it's daylight tomorrow. We'll get there about 8:00 a.m." So we waited with Joel in terrible pain all during the night, not knowing what kind of permanent damage it would do, or even if he would live. At 8:00 I heard the plane coming so I went down to the airstrip and Anne stayed with Joel. As soon as the plane landed, Dr. Neva rushed up to the house. Anne said, "He hasn't cried for about half an hour." The doctor examined him. Apparently the hernia had rectified itself after about 18 hours. We flew on out and took him to the surgeon who immediately did surgery. He said it was just amazing that Joel didn't get gangrene during all that time.

We thank God that he took care of our kids, in those, and many, many other situations when they could easily have been taken. We attribute their lives to God's grace, His loving-kindness, and His plan for us and for our children.

Bob, Lorna, Joel and Daniel

The Saga of Echobe

As told by Anne

When we first went to San Pedro, don Abram, who was the *patron* of about 70 Sirionó people, assigned us two helpers. Echobe was Perry's language assistant and his sweet little wife, Petrona,

was my helper in the home. During the first year of translation, as Perry and Echobe worked together on the book of Mark, Echobe came to learn of the power that Jesus has over the elements, sickness, and the evil spirits. During that year he and Petrona both put their trust in the Lord.

Echobe helped us for many years. Later, we moved to Ibiato and when we went back to visit San Pedro a few years

Echobe and Petrona

later we saw that Echobe had an enormous growth on his jaw. As time went on it became larger and an ulcer developed on the tumor. He found it more and more difficult to swallow. We decided to take him to the doctor in Riberalta to see what could be done for him. The doctor in Riberalta did not give us any encouragement so we decided to take him to Cochabamba.

Perry was the mission field director at that time, so we decided I should be the one to take Echobe to Cochabamba. I took him to see the doctor, who upon examining him, told me that he could do surgery, but would have to take out the whole left jaw, cut out one of his ribs, and graft it in to form a new jaw. He wasn't sure if Echobe would be able to eat normally, because in doing the surgery they might have to cut muscles and nerves that would affect the movement of his tongue and jaw. Of course, for the Sirionó, meat is the most important part of their diet. It all sounded terrible to me, so I asked him if he had ever done this surgery before. He told me he had, once, and I blatantly asked if the patient had lived. He answered that he had lived three months. I told him that because of the uncertainties involved we needed a few days to decide whether or not to proceed with surgery.

We had prayed and prayed over the matter before going to Cochabamba and we had felt that the Lord wanted us to do this. Bob and Lois Wilkinson were a real tower of strength to me during these days, praying with me, and encouraging me. I called Perry by radio and told him what the doctor had said. Perry tried to encourage me, but he left the decision up to me. This was a very, very difficult time because Echobe wanted to go ahead with the surgery, but he knew nothing of what was involved, so it was as though I was the one to decide if he should die or live.

The Scripture was so precious to me during those days of decision. This is what I wrote as I was seeking guidance, "Romans 15:13 has been so precious to me, 'May the God of hope fill you with all joy and peace as you trust in him, so that you may overflow with hope by the power of the Holy Spirit.' God is the one giving me hope for Echobe and as I believe, I have joy and peace through the power of the Holy Spirit. Then yesterday I came across Romans 15:4, 5. One needs patience in the matter of hope. I guess the Lord knows I need time for my faith to grow. Anyway, it says that God is the God of patience, too, as well as hope. Then it says that hope comes from the comfort of the Scriptures. Boy, I've found that true. As long as I'm in the Word I have hope."

The first night after talking with the doctor and not knowing whether to go ahead with the surgery or not, the verse that I read was Psalm 143:8, "Show me the way I should go..." As I prayed this prayer over and over during the next week, the assurance came that we should go ahead with surgery. The morning of surgery I read Psalm 16:7, "I will praise the Lord, who counsels me..." The next weeks were a time of holding onto this in faith.

Meanwhile, Echobe was very, very anemic and weak, so they put him in the hospital and began to give him blood. Perry and others from Tumi Chucua donated blood and sent it to Cochabamba for them to use. People in Cochabamba also donated. The hospital was a good distance from our mission house, so Bob Wilkinson would take me to the hospital each morning on his motorcycle and I would stay with Echobe, then in the afternoon I would come home in a *micro*. This was indeed a stretching time of faith for me. I saw so many things that I felt were not done correctly there in the hospital. Once the needle came out of Echobe's arm and fell on the floor and they picked it up and stuck it back in. Again and again I had to turn everything over to the Lord and trust Him rather than any man.

All during this time Echobe was very dependent on me because he spoke Sirionó and very little Spanish and so I was his lifeline. After the first night Echobe wanted to leave the hospital, but eventually he became more accustomed to being there. We began to read from the Sirionó Scriptures and he seemed to drink them in. Some verses that meant a lot to both of us were Hebrews 13:5, 6, "God has said, 'Never will I leave you; never will I forsake you.' So we say with confidence, 'The Lord is my helper; I will not be afraid. What can man do to me?'" What a comfort that was.

The day came for the surgery, and I prayed with Echobe before he went in. Finally they came and called me and said that the surgery was successful; I could go see him. He was still in the hall outside the operation theater. His head and face were completely swathed in bandages. My heart was paralyzed by fear and I thought, "Oh, I've killed him," because I truly felt that I was the one responsible for this. I went to him and called softly, "Echobe?" From those bandages came the sweetest sound imaginable—a gentle chuckle of pleasure to hear the voice of someone he knew and loved.

The days ahead were not easy. One night I had a terrible nightmare that he had died. I awoke with my heart beating wildly. There was no hope of sleep now. Then I took out the Word and began to read, and as the Lord had done so many times before, He spoke to my heart and quieted it and I slept. We had to give Echobe baby food to eat as he couldn't eat regular food. A friend of our son Daniel, from Food for the Hungry, had a surplus of baby food and he had heard about Echobe. He asked if Echobe could use some of the baby food; he donated a large amount. Even with the baby food, it was difficult for Echobe to eat as he had to lie back to be able to swallow. Perry thought up the idea of putting the food in a squeeze bottle and squeezing the food into his mouth. This worked wonderfully.

Because of a transportation strike, Bob Wilkinson would take me to the hospital, but when it was time to go home I had to go out and flag down a ride with whatever kind soul would stop and pick me up. Sometimes when they let me out I had to walk a good many miles to get to the mission house.

One side of Echobe's mouth was sunken in and the doctor said he needed to do further surgery and take some muscle from his gluteus to repair the mouth. Praise the Lord that the doctor did all his work *gratis*. However, the doctor fell and broke his leg before the surgery could be done so it was postponed quite a while. Don Samuel, the Bolivian buyer for our mission, was a great help to us during this time. Since the surgery was postponed, I left Echobe in Cochabamba and returned to Tumi Chucua to visit Perry and Joel. Don Samuel would visit Echobe, take him out on trips to the market, and buy medicine for him.

After the second surgery, there were infections that would not clear up, even with antibiotics. The doctor told us he didn't know what to do about it. This was very discouraging. One night when I woke up and was worried about it, the thought came, "The Lord has given us so many promises and has answered so many prayers for the surgery and for healing. All during that time I had told the Lord again and again that I was trusting Him, not medicine or doctors, so now again I was just going to ask and believe Him to give healing from the infection." The verses the Lord gave us during this time were Psalm 27:14, "Wait for the Lord; be strong and take heart..." and Hebrews 10:36, "You need to persevere so that when you have done the will of God, you will receive what he has promised."

All the infection finally dried up. God is the great physician!

Three months went by, Echobe was still alive. Years went by, Echobe was still alive. Echobe would never win a beauty contest, but when we went back to visit over 20 years later there was Echobe's sweet smiling face waiting to greet us! He had been able to live a fairly normal life. God is Faithful! The surgery was done in 1979. Echobe lived until 2003.

Are You Ready?

One night Joel, about five years old, and I were lying on the bed, talking about the second coming of Christ. I asked him, "Would you like it if Jesus should come back tonight?"

As a missionary kid, Joel had moved around often. Still, I didn't expect his answer. "No, I haven't packed up yet."

"You don't need to pack up. You just need to be ready by believing in Jesus with all your heart."

"Oh, then I'm ready because Jesus is my Savior, and He's in my heart."

Anne was in the kitchen, so Joel called out, "Mama, are you ready if Jesus comes back tonight?"

"Yes, I'm ready."

"Are you trusting Jesus as your Savior?" he persisted.

"Yes."

"Oh, that's gooood!"

From Darkness to Light

As told by a Sirionó man

"Pray to it!" they said. "Pray to the skull of your relative. Ask it to make you well. Ask it to send wild game so you'll have something to eat." That's the way I was taught when I was a boy. We didn't know about God. Nobody told us. We prayed only to the skulls and arm bones of our relatives. When someone died, we would build a platform and leave him on it. After several moons, we would come back and search for the skull and arm bones. In cold weather we would keep them warm so they would help us.

A few years ago the missionaries, Eoco (Tall-one) and Señora, came. Right after that I was very sick—so sick I could not sit up. They went upriver to see me. They prayed for me to a God they said lived up in the sky. For many months they gave me medicines.

After I improved and after they learned the language better, they told me a story I couldn't believe. It was about someone who was killed and after being dead three days, made himself alive again. I couldn't believe that. I've seen many deaths, but I've never seen anyone live again after death. They also told me that I would live again if I believed in that one. I wanted to believe, but it was so new to me. Finally, after a long time I believed, then I knew that the message was true. Then I started going to classes to learn to read. I made a rope and traded it to Eoco for the reading primer.

But reading was too hard; I never did learn.

Then lots of books came to us. These were the Word of God. I enjoyed listening and asking questions as I heard so many new things from God's Word.

After Eoco left, we continued to have meetings. At the meetings, everyone who knows Jesus prays. It used to be that we did many things to appease the evil spirits. It used to be that we prayed to the skulls of the dead. Now we pray to God.

Did He Die Again?

As Daniel's last fling before going to the USA for his senior year of high school, he and I took a two-week trip to preach and teach God's Word.

We went by canoe to El Carmen, where we stayed in the home of one of the believers. Several people there had a real hunger for God's Word. One was Maria, a woman who had received the Lord several years before. After her conversion, the husband "cast her off" to take a younger wife. After a year or so, the new wife died, and the husband wanted to reunite with Maria. Maria was so poor she sometimes didn't know where her next meal would come from. Here was her chance to have a husband to provide for her. But no, she told him, "Because of Christ I forgive all that you've done to me. But I can't become your wife again unless you put your trust in Christ and agree to establish a Christian home." He wasn't agreeable to that, so Maria continued as a poor widow, but living a life of triumph in Christ.

In El Carmen we got an old, leaky dugout canoe, which we patched with rags and mud. We paddled downriver for a day and a half, visiting people along the way, until we arrived at Irobe. We hadn't seen the people there for twelve years, but they still remembered some of the songs and Biblical truths we had told them.

A few days later we went by foot to another village a few hours away. As I talked to one old man there, a former chief, I told him that God's son Jesus had died as payment for our sins. Surprised, he asked, "Did he die again?" He remembered that we had told him years before of Jesus' death, and he thought I was bringing more recent news.

It was a joy to tell him that Jesus had died once for all for our sins—death no more has dominion over Him. He arose from the grave. He's alive forevermore; He loves us and prays for us, and wants us to trust Him. The old man agreed with all I said, but how hard it is for those who have walked all their lives in darkness to come to light and life in Christ.

Bananas

"Which of you fathers, if your son asks for a fish,
will give him a snake instead?"

Bananas are one of my favorite foods. As a child, my mama would regularly send me to the little country store in Troy, Mississippi with a bucket of eggs to exchange for groceries. Mr. Tommy would often have a stalk of bananas hanging there, and he'd remove each banana very carefully. How good they were.

When I went to college, I got a job on Saturdays in the produce department of what was probably the first supermarket in Columbia, South Carolina. I'd go to work too early for breakfast, and arrive back at the college too late for supper. But since it was the weekend, we were to throw away all the fruit and vegetables that would not look good by Monday. The only thing we could take for ourselves were the very ripe bananas. So I'd take a large bag of bananas, and eat them all as I walked the fourteen blocks back to school late Saturday night. A meal of bananas was my main food on Saturdays, and I never tired of it.

In Bolivia I raised bananas in our back yard, so we nearly always had a big stalk hanging on our porch. That was often the snack for the kids between meals.

One morning for family devotions, our reading included the verse, "Which of you fathers, if your son asks for a fish, will give him a snake instead?" (Luke 11:11). Little Daniel immediately answered, "No, my dad wouldn't do that. He'd just say, 'There are plenty of bananas on the back porch.'"

Pets

Lots of birds and animals have "graced" our lives, especially when our "kids" were kids—monkey, agouti, capybara, alligator, deer, parrot, ostrich, as well as the usual dogs, cats, and guinea pigs.

Lorna loved cats, especially Misifú. Each time we flew in the small Helio or Cessna between Tumi Chucua and the Sirionó area, we'd put Misifú in a basket and fasten the lid. Sometimes she cried loudly, and might have caused a crash if she had gotten out of the basket. Once, when we got to our destination, we opened the basket, and there were four cats instead of one!

Joel loved dogs and he had a boxer named Butch. But dogs were not allowed in the Children's Home. So while Anne and I were in the Sirionó village of Ibiato, and Joel in school at Tumi Chucua, he would go once a week to another house to cook up a week's supply of rice and meat for Butch. One time his friend Mickey was helping him cook the dog food. It smelled pretty good, so they dared each other to taste it. They liked the dog food; they ate it; they enjoyed it.

That night at the Children's Home Aunt Marge served rice and meat. Aunt Marge didn't feel complimented when Mickey, in all innocence, said, "This is almost as good as Butch's food!" They had a lot of explaining to do.

Bob and Daniel had Pedro, a pet deer which had been brought to us as a baby. He was lots of fun and would follow any of us around when we were outside—that is, until he became a "teenager." He began to wander to other people's homes and out into the forest. As the Sirionó hunters kill anything that moves in the forest, we, and they, became concerned for his safety. So Pedro wore a big red ribbon around his neck. Sometimes he brought his *novia* out into the clearing where we could see her. But she'd never follow him all the way to our house. Finally he disappeared; I guess they eloped.

But it was Oscar who was our favorite pet, at least during his first year. Oscar was a rhea, or South American ostrich. He was given to us as a baby by one of the hunters. His mom had already gone into the cooking pot. We fed him some of our own food, such as bananas and bits of meat, but even as a baby he could find food for himself—worms, grasshoppers, and other insects, even lizards and snakes as he grew.

When it was time for us to go to Tumi Chucua for a few months, we took Oscar with us on the plane. Everyone there seemed to enjoy him. Most of the people—missionaries and nationals—had never seen an ostrich, as ostriches live in the grasslands, or pampas, and Tumi Chucua is located in the rainforest, so he was popular that first year.

At one year old, he was six feet tall, and since he had never seen another ostrich, he must have thought he was a person. He liked to be with people but didn't like to be touched. If he saw a group standing and talking together, he'd walk right up and join the circle, always looking at whoever was talking.

Once Oscar even led the school parade. The school children had made paper lanterns with candles inside; the parade was at night, with candles lit. Oscar saw them coming, and went to meet them. When he got a few feet away, he turned and walked the other way, and for all the world it looked like he was the parade master.

Anne feeding Oscar

Oscar didn't need any help in finding food. But he also liked you to feed him bananas, and it was fun to watch the whole banana slowly make its way down the three-foot esophagus. At first we'd peal the banana; as he grew he would swallow it unpeeled. He was worse than a billy goat for eating things he shouldn't. He'd peck at the buttons on your clothes. Even earrings weren't exempt. As people went to the lake to bathe and swim he'd eat their soap—once even a washcloth. He'd eat plastic bags hung on a clothesline (missionaries were among the first great recyclers). He'd knock people's papayas off the trees. He was accused of eating little watermelons off the vines, and even the blooms, so there was no harvest.

Oscar became so unruly and disobedient that we knew we had to get rid of him. A lady upriver begged for him. We explained to her that Oscar might cost her friendships and relationships with neighbors. But she insisted she had a large, open pasture and he would be safe there. Se we caught Oscar, restrained him with burlap, and put him on a river launch. On the way, he hit his head and died before reaching his final destination. The lady comforted us as she assured us she'd given him a proper burial with a tombstone and flowers.

Goodbye, Oscar. I wish you and your mom had been left in the pampas.

Germ Warfare or International Relations?

One day, in 1974, I was sitting on a bench watching a soccer match. Two young boys, maybe six years old, came and sat next to me. One was white. One was brown. They were friends. One was an MK (missionary kid); the other was from one of the many indigenous groups of Bolivia. The MK knew how to whistle loudly by inserting two fingers in his mouth, and blowing hard. He was trying to teach his buddy to whistle. He kept demonstrating. Then he put his same two fingers in his friend's mouth, and said, "Blow hard." But no whistle came out. Then he told his friend, "Put your two fingers in my mouth. I'll blow and you'll learn." I was intrigued as I watched them for maybe half an hour or more. I did think of giving them a lesson on not sharing their germs with each other. But what gusto and camaraderie!! And what are a few hundred germs among good friends?

The Honeymoon

The Sirionó call the month of June the "fat month," as that's when the wild animals are fattest and the honeycombs fullest. So June is vacation month. They divide up into groups of four or five families and spend a couple of weeks deep in the forest, camping out, hunting and eating primarily wild pig, deer, agouti, tapir, and honey. They have names for fourteen species of honeybees which produce good honey.

There was a double wedding the night before the people set off for the forest on their vacation. Early the next morning they left. Our sons Bob and Daniel also went, and they were in the same group as the newlyweds and parents. Everyone had plenty to eat and a grand time, including the honeymooners. We teased Bob and Daniel, still teenagers, about already having had their honeymoon.

Years later when Bob and Kersten married and started on their honeymoon, Bob said to her, "Guess I have to confess one thing to you. This isn't the first honeymoon I've ever been on."

I never did find out what Kersten's reaction was to that!

Rites of Passage

Our sons Bob and Daniel returned to Bolivia to be with us for the summer of 1978. We spent most of the summer in Ibiato with the Sirionó. The boys always enjoyed camping, hunting, and fishing with the people.

Near the end of the summer it was time for all of us to return to Tumi Chucua, the mission headquarters, and for Bob to return to school in the USA (Daniel stayed on in Bolivia for a year). So that we would only need one flight, the boys decided to go by foot to San Joaquin, where they felt they could catch a river launch to Brazil, then a road to Tumi Chucua. Anne and I were doubtful; they insisted they needed a long trek, and wanted to have a last fling by themselves, maybe to convince themselves and us that they were now responsible adults. We agreed, with some reservations, to let them do this, as we knew there would be some hardships. They planned to walk about 35 kilometers north then about 60 kilometers northeast, to reach San Joaquin. The first leg of the journey might not be too bad, as it was open pampa and not many swamps or streams to cross. The Sirionó told them that the last leg would be through numerous swamps, some very deep. Many years before, there was a way to get through the swamps, but apparently nobody had taken that route for over a generation. And what of the alligators, anacondas, wild pigs, and anything else that they might encounter?

They set off with their supplies, including trail mix, cookies, matches, oatmeal, a rifle, knife, cooking pot, and backpacks, with Chiro (my translation assistant) escorting them the first two days. We wondered if we'd ever see them again, but we knew they liked to hike and were very familiar with the forest, swamps, and pampas.

The second or third day, as they waded through a swampy area, a large anaconda swam right by them, not a yard away.

They arrived at a big water hole that had begun to dry up. Daniel said, "Hundreds and hundreds of birds—cranes, batos, cabeza secas, spoon-billed flamingos—were feeding there. They didn't fly until we were very close. Then we passed through a patch of scrub and there must have been 50 capybaras there. They didn't see us until we got close. Then they let out those loud snorts—some ran into the scrub and others into the water. We didn't wait for them to come out as they can submerge for a long time!

"I don't remember all the places we slept, but we slept at several ranches. At one place, the owner told us he knew Dad. We were treated very well there. At another place we slept in the yard. Bob's pants had lots of mud on them, so he hung them out to dry. The next day, dressed in his underwear, he would scrape the dry mud off the pants with a hunting knife, and then give them a shake with the knife still in his hand. At one point the knife escaped his grasp and went into his knee—not a long cut, but deep. We knew it would get stiff fairly soon, so we changed plans, headed west toward the big Mamore River, canceling our plans to wade through the swamps toward San Joaquin. The owner gave us horses and a guide to take us about three hours toward the Mamore River. From there we started out on foot and Bob hobbled along. After a while he tied a string to his foot, as his leg was aching. The string helped him pull his foot forward with each step. After a long trek, the leg was hurting so badly that he sat down on the ground. I tried to make him comfortable, then I ran west to try to find a ranch and get horses. There was a jeep at the ranch, so men went with me in the jeep to pick up Bob. They had cattle penicillin at the ranch, so they treated Bob with that. They gave us a room to stay in. After a few days Bob felt better so we told them that we would head out to the river by foot, but the rancher had his men take us in the vehicle for several miles. Then we trekked on toward the Mamore River.

"When we got near the river, we met an old man and woman who lived in a little thatched roofed house. From there we walked to the river each day, a mile or so away and sat there for hours hoping to flag down a launch going toward Brazil. After a couple of days our food ran out, so the old man and I went hunting with the rifle, part of the time in the forest and part on the edge of the river. All we found were a bunch of turtle eggs and three seagull eggs. Bob, who was always clever, exclaimed over the seagull eggs, saying they were his favorite. Of course that was because he could never stomach turtle eggs. At supper, when he cracked open the boiled eggs; they had the beginning of baby birds in them. The lady exclaimed over them, saying they are the best that way! Anyway, Bob did eat them!"

Bob told us, "The old woman enjoyed telling jokes, but she had lots of missing teeth, and I couldn't understand her. I did laugh just to be polite. Later Daniel told me I shouldn't have laughed, as all her jokes were vulgar!"

After sitting at the river for two or three days they caught a ride on a boat going to Brazil.

During those 15 or more days that Anne and I didn't see our boys, we wondered whether we should have let them go on such a dangerous adventure. But when we heard all their stories, saw how well they took care of each other, and made the right decisions, we were glad to see they were on the way toward becoming responsible adults.

Afterward, we realized that our estimate of about 90 kilometers to San Joaquin was way too low. We were glad they made the decision to go instead to the Mamore River and flag a river boat to take them to Brazil.

We laughed when they told us that somewhere along the way, Daniel, at least 12 pounds lighter than Bob, carried him across at least one swamp to protect the knee wound from the dirty water. Then he had to cross the swamp again to get their loads.

Bob recently told us, "Although I don't remember all the details of the trip, I do remember feeling great about the adventure of it all, and that you and Mom were willing to let us do this, and a great sense of accomplishment that we were able to complete the trip—confronting the challenges as they arose."

Memorable Birthday

*Everyone beyond threescore and ten should have had
a few special, memorable birthdays.*

In some ways, 1971 was the hardest year of my life. The Bolivian government, following Chile's lead, had become very communistic, anti-religion, and anti-American. A national campaign was in progress to indoctrinate the whole populace into Marxism. It was a very difficult time for everyone who didn't embrace the new dogma—churches and missions were attacked, especially those related in any way to USA. All over the capital and other cities were posted big pictures of the USA flag in the form of a pig, and with ugly inscriptions.

The campaign was orchestrated from the top and with much success. Even our closest friends were afraid to befriend us. It was difficult to renew residence permits, licenses, and airplane registrations.

Russia, Cuba, and Chile were *in*. The USA, westerners, people of religion and evangelical missionaries were *out*. It looked as though missionaries would be forced to leave.

A second, but related, problem was a lawsuit. Some influential men had borrowed several hundred thousand dollars from international lending organizations to set up a sugar/alcohol factory near our headquarters; over five hundred acres of sugar cane was ready for harvest. But the processing equipment ordered from Europe hadn't arrived. The cane would soon spoil. What could they do? One night over 400 acres of cane mysteriously burned up, and our mission workers were accused. Even though no evidence pointed to us, they brought a lawsuit.

With the political climate against foreigners and people of religion, it looked like we would lose the case. They talked about taking over our airplanes, vehicles, homes, mission headquarters, and any other assets. As field director, I was put under a restraining order—not allowed to travel outside the mission headquarters area.

In August of that year, as my birthday was just a couple of weeks away, Anne asked what I'd like as a present. I answered, "There are three things I'd like, but only the Lord can give them to me. I'm praying that this Communist government will topple, that we win this unjust lawsuit, and that I be released as field director of the mission to go back to the Sirionó work."

Can you believe that just days before my August 13 birthday, the Bolivian Military staged a *coup d'etat* and set up a new government that promoted freedom of expression and freedom of religion.

With that, the plaintiffs saw the handwriting on the wall, and the lawsuit was dropped. And then, that same week, at field conference, our missionaries agreed to let me go back to the Sirionó area to finish the Sirionó New Testament translation!

Now I ask, is God sufficient? Able? Does he care? Does he answer prayer? Is he the Lord of the harvest?

I'll always remember my forty-first birthday when I saw God's love, God's power, and God's wisdom demonstrated in wonderful ways.

A Day in the Life of a Bible Translator

The two-way radio is our principal link with the outside world, so this morning as usual, we enjoyed our five-minute contact with our headquarters, and also listened during breakfast to several of the other translation teams.

Just after the radio schedules ended, Yande, one of the Sirionó men, came over with his broken gun for me to repair. These people, who have used bow and arrow for centuries, now use guns, too, but they still haven't learned to take care of them. I told him to leave the gun and I'd look at it later.

My morning was spent in working on a translation of parts of Mark 7. One of the spots that gives difficulty is verse 15. ("Nothing outside a man can make him 'unclean' by going into him. Rather, it is what comes out of a man that makes him 'unclean.'") The wording "going into him" must be made a little more specific, as the Sirionó might understand this as referring to a thorn, arrow, or skin-worms. The verse now reads, "Nothing that a person puts into his mouth makes him unclean; it is the things that come out from underneath his heart that make him unclean." Verses 21 and 22 also needed adaptations, since the Sirionó do not speak of theft, murder, deceit, and other abstract nouns, but rather of "to steal, to kill people, and to deceive people."

After lunch I began work on the gun. Just as I had it all torn apart, a man was brought to us who had a serious cut on his hand. It was fortunate that it had happened only fifty yards or so from our house, as it was bleeding badly. Several veins and arteries and one large tendon had been cut. It took us almost two hours to get the blood stopped and sew up the gaping wound (16 stitches).

During the procedure, several people came for medicines but were told to come back later. As we were taking care of the man, I noticed a scar on his other arm and asked how it had happened. He said, "The same way as this wound; my wife did it." Today they had been fighting over tobacco, and she had cut him with a machete. (Lord, you know better than we the wickedness of the human heart. Help us to be good witnesses to these people, who need you so much.)

Bob and Daniel, who were very young at the time, were impressed with the "operation," and especially with people who fight with knives. Daniel said, "Don't these people know they are supposed to love God?" Bob said, "When I get grown I'm not going to get married; I'm going to stay single so I can go everywhere preaching." (Lord, help our children to see how terrible sin is, and may their love for you continue to grow.)

A little later Julio came from upriver with a message from an old woman whose husband had just died. Both the old man and woman were professing believers, and she had sent Julio to ask whether she should put a wooden cross on the husband's grave as a marker.

After Julio left, Antonio came in from the hunt with a deer. Since he was using my gun, he gave us a nice piece of venison.

After two or three more short visits from Sirionó and other people, we had supper and a little rest before our night literacy classes. My class of men practiced mostly the few sentences of the crucifixion story that each will read at the meeting Sunday night. (Lord, help them to learn to read well, that they might read and understand your Word.)

Sirionó man

God's Word at Work

After we finished translating the first draft of 1 John, Humberto agreed to work with me for a few days to help polish it up, making the message clearer and more natural. He was a help, but he liked to talk about his sickness, aches, and pains. One morning he came in cradling one hand in the other, saying, "My hand hurts." I ignored his comment, as I wanted to get down to work. After we had worked for a few minutes, he again said, "My hand hurts." No comment from me. After the third time, I asked what the problem was. "My wife and I had a fight, and she bit my hand. Here, you can see the teeth marks, and it really hurts."

At that point, we had arrived in 1 John chapter 4 verses 10 and 11. "This is love: not that we loved God, but that he loved us and sent his Son as an atoning sacrifice for our sins. Dear friends, since God so loved us, we also ought to love one another." We discussed the meaning of these verses, and how they should affect our relationship to others, and specifically to our wives.

After a few minutes he walked out; I thought he was going to the toilet.

Finally he came back with a big grin on his face. He said, "I went home and told my wife what God's Word says. We apologized to each other and agreed we now want to walk in God's way."

What a thrill it is to see how God works when His Word is translated into the mother tongue.

My Friend, the Enemy

Two groups of feuding people, transformed through Christ,
find that they can love one another.

"Feed the enemy people?" Chiro couldn't believe what he was hearing.

The Sirionó and Ayore people of Bolivia have been death-dealing enemies for generations. The Sirionó word for Ayore is "enemy," and they even felt the Ayore had supernatural powers.

After my Sirionó translation assistant, Chiro, and his family arrived at Tumi Chucua for the annual leadership training course, I learned that three Ayore men were also coming. Since they could not bring their wives, the director asked me if Chiro and his wife, Nanci, would feed the men in their home during the next three months, if we would provide the food.

One day I casually told Chiro about the Ayore men who would be coming.

"Are they going to study in the same course we will be in?" Chiro, a new Christian, asked in alarm.

"Yes," I said, "but they know Jesus now, just like you, and they will be studying here at Tumi Chucua. In fact, they are not bringing their wives, so they need somebody to cook their meals. I've been asked if you and Nanci would cook for them and feed them if we provide the food."

Feed the enemy people? How could Chiro ask his wife to do this? He squirmed an excuse. "I doubt that she'll be willing to feed them." So I told him to talk to Nanci, pray about it and let me know their decision.

The following day when Chiro didn't mention the subject, I asked him if he'd talked to his wife. "No," came the slow reply. "I haven't talked to her about it." Then he hit on a compromise plan. "If you won't tell her that they are enemy people, I think maybe she would be willing to cook for them."

"No, Chiro," I replied. "I don't think that's the way you should do it. You and Nanci should talk it over and decide if you really want to do this as a service to the Lord."

During the next few days Chiro battled it out in his heart. Because he was a new creature in Christ he really wanted to help the Ayore men; but the generations of hatred, animosities, and warfare between the two peoples struggled with his new nature. He wondered, "What will the people in my village think if they learn I've been associating with the enemy people—if they learn I've been feeding them in my house?" Finally, however, he surrendered to the Lord, saying, "Yes, we will be glad to feed the enemy people."

When the Ayore men arrived, Chiro and Nanci graciously accepted them into their home. A few days later Chiro exclaimed to me, "You know, those Ayore are the most wonderful Christians! They stay up until midnight reading their Bible, singing, and praying. I've never seen anything like it!"

About the same time, the missionary with the Ayore reported that the three Ayore men had said the same thing about Chiro and Nanci. In His own wonderful way God had removed any faults the former enemies might have seen in each other, and they had found only the good.

When Chiro and Nanci returned to their home in Ibiato they told the other Sirionó that the enemy people really weren't supernatural, as they had always believed. The old myths about the Ayore being evil spirits just weren't true.

Of the twelve different language groups who participated in the course, the Ayore are now probably the favorites of the Sirionó. When they are apart they include in their letters, "Send my greetings to the enemy people."

A couple of years later, Chiro heard that a road was being built between Trinidad and Santa Cruz and would come within a mile of our village. He was happy. I asked why. His answer: "So I can go and visit my friends the enemy people."

History doesn't reveal where the hatreds and fears came from, but one thing is sure—the power of Christ in Sirionó and Ayore lives has changed them. Now they're no longer enemies, but brothers in Christ.

Translation Treasures

When the Sirionó hunters come in with game, the women are said to "jump at the meat." This figure of speech is used quite effectively in translating Mark 7:9 "observe your own traditions." The Sirionó translation says "Unfortunately you leave the Word of God, and you continually jump for the word of your ancestors."

The Sirionó language is rich in figures of speech, which are consequently used very generously in the translation of the Scriptures. Instead of saying, as in English, "their eyes were heavy," the Sirionó version of Mark 14:40 is "their eyes were biting." Both are figures of speech, each meaning to its hearers "they were sleepy."

To the Sirionó, a person who has a hard heart is one who is hard to kill. Obviously this figure of speech used in the English Bible would not give the proper meaning if translated literally into Sirionó.

The Sirionó and I worked for days on a translation of "the first commandment." The Biblical concept of "first" in this context seems to be "first in importance or rank," but the Sirionó word for "first" means only "first in time or space." After I had explained many times as best I could what "the first commandment" is, the Sirionó finally said "Oh, the hip (or trunk) of the commandments." Since the hip or trunk to the Sirionó is the most important part of a thing, the scribe says in Mark 12:28 "Which is the hip of the commandments?"

Finishing the New Testament

Dear Heavenly Father,

Today I hold in my hands a copy of the Sirionó New Testament—complete and beautifully printed and bound. And now I lay it at your feet and say, "Thank You." Thank you for your faithfulness, for your love, for your patience with me. Thank you for letting me have a small part in this beautiful book.

I do not understand why you chose me. Why did you let me finish this New Testament while others became sick and had to go home? Why did you keep me from giving up and going back? I wanted to, time and again, you know.

Father, I know it is not because of who I am. It is rather because of who You are. You choose. You chose Jacob the deceiver rather than his brother Esau. You chose Paul the persecutor. You chose Peter the denier. You chose my fellow missionaries in Bolivia, some weak as I. You use our frailties to show your greatness.

Thank you for letting me be one of hundreds of people whom you used to complete this book. Thank you for Meliton and Ecuataya who taught me the language, and for all the other Sirionó who corrected and encouraged. Thank you for raising up Sirionó believers such as Echobe and Chiro who so willingly helped to put your Word into their very own language. Thank you for the bilingual school teachers who taught their own people to read this book.

Thank you for a wife who carried the extra load—making primers, teaching, teacher training, hymn writing, medical work—to keep me translating. Thank you for our children and for their prayers for the Sirionó and for the translation.

Thank you for wonderful pilots to fly us to and from the Sirionó villages—men who really care about Sirionós and translators. Thank you for typists and printers. For radio men. For school teachers and Children's Home parents. Thank you for the love and encouragement of fellow missionaries.

Thank you especially for all those who prayed. Thank you for Mr. and Mrs. Atkins, who have prayed for us every day for 22 years. Thank you for churches and individuals in Mississippi,

Memphis, Columbia, and elsewhere who through prayer have had a part in producing this beautiful book.

Father, there are so many I can't name them all. But thank you, too, for those of your children who have given sacrificially in order to bring to reality our dream of a Sirionó New Testament. For the World Home Bible League, who has paid for all printing costs for this publication. For Mary Spence, who has so faithfully printed and mailed our form letters. For friends around the world. For all others who year by year have been your source to supply all our needs.

How many people does it take to finish a New Testament? I don't know, Father. You keep the records. I know when I see your beautiful tapestry some day I will be only one small thread running through a sea of color and harmony representing Bible translation around the world. Thank you for letting me, by your grace, have a part. Thank you for choosing me. I love you! I worship you! I praise you!

Perry Priest
(*adapted from a letter by Millie Larson*)

Going Down!

We had a very precious experience that brought us so close to Jesus Christ on January 14, 1983. We had just finished translating and printing selected Psalms and Proverbs in the Sirionó language.

Anne and I had gone out to Ibiato. We had been there 10 days and had had a nice "Bible Conference," teaching Psalms and Proverbs each night. Our pilot, Jeff[1], was bringing Anne and me back to Cochabamba from Ibiato. We had to cross the Andes mountains, including many very high peaks. Since the weather was bad, the pilot went up to 18,500 feet. All three of us were taking oxygen through a tube. He was flying by instruments, as visibility was zero.

Several things happened almost at once. The station in La Paz, that helped him to know about where he was, suddenly went off the air. Then we hit very rough weather and the plane was really rocking. Then the motor conked out. Since Jeff couldn't see the horizon he couldn't tell if his wings were horizontal. The right wing all at once dipped. We started going down so fast my stomach was in my mouth. Our pilot reported emergency and power failure and did everything he could think of to get power but we kept descending fast. Once or twice the motor caught but only for a few seconds. We were down to 13,000 feet in what seemed like two or three minutes. Jeff said we were going to crash. I said to the Lord, "That's okay. I've asked you many times in the past not to take me till our kids are grown and until the Sirionó work is done, and you've answered, and now we are ready." I figured our kids didn't need us anymore, and we had just had good meetings with the Sirionó and they didn't need us any more. And we'd had such a nice visit with all the US family in November and with Daniel and his wife Jhenny in December. So I thanked the Lord for sparing our lives for all that time, for the wonderful life we'd had, and told Him that we were now ready, that it was nice we could go together, and that we'd be seeing Him at any moment now. Then I turned around to Anne who was on the back seat and told her we'd be in heaven soon.

---

[1] A pseudonym has been used.

I had taught the Sirionó from Psalms that the Lord is our Refuge, like a den where animals can go for safety. And the thought came that the Lord is just as much my Refuge in the clouds heading for a mountain crash as when everything is more to my liking. I had real peace and felt, "If this is what it's like to know you are going to die in one moment, it isn't bad." I did pray for all of my kids, that they would grow strong in the Lord and put Him first. My saddest thought was for Jeff's wife and their children.

We had just gotten 10 or 12 days' of mail, so had been reading the letters during the first hour of the flight—very nice letters from my mother, our children, as well as a good many others. So one thought I had was "Wouldn't it be nice to answer these letters and tell them how much we love and appreciate them, and how much we enjoyed their letters, before we go."

I'm not sure how so many thoughts and prayers went through my mind so fast. Somewhere along the way I heard Jeff say on the radio to give his greetings to his wife and then he said, "Perry sends greetings to everyone and says to tell them we'll see them in heaven." I thought that was really funny as we had hardly talked at all, and I hadn't told him to say that, but then I decided that was a good message and I was happy with it.

Jeff was doing a good job keeping the plane upright, although it was rocking and dropping fast. I was constantly watching the altimeter, and when we got down to 11,500 feet, I felt sure we were about ready to hit a mountain peak.

Jeff had been turning and pulling several knobs and switches, and when we got down to 11,500 feet, all at once the engine started and we began to climb at full power. So we steadily climbed up and went back to Trinidad, over an hour away. He had turned around and headed that way when the engine first failed, knowing that the highest mountains had been just ahead of us toward Cochabamba. After we landed, Jeff handed me the keys. He said, "I'll never be a pilot again." I said, "Well, keep the keys anyway until tomorrow and I'll see what I can do."

The problem was that we had run out of gas in one tank and normally there's no problem in switching, but with the sudden turbulent weather, and the La Paz station suddenly off the air, he had simply forgotten to switch tanks and thought it was engine failure, and it was only when we got down to 11,500 feet that he realized what the problem was. By that time we were probably below some of the nearby peaks, but because of the rain and stormy weather, visibility was almost zero, so we'll never know for sure. We just thanked the Lord for His safety.

We spent that night and most of the next day in Trinidad, as the weather stayed bad. Jeff was very discouraged. The reason we had the problem was that he had been used to flying a different plane. He got his gauges a little bit mixed up and he thought he had both gas tanks on, but one of the tanks was off and when he finally realized that and turned it on we had no more problems. He said anybody that can do that shouldn't be flying. But he got a lot of encouragement afterwards. The chief pilot told me later, "You know, if he hadn't been a good pilot, and without being able to see anything, no orientation, the horizon or anything, he would never have gotten that plane straightened out again." He's still flying planes. He's one of the few pilots that we had in Bolivia that never had an accident. But it could have been the other way except for God's grace.

We got off the next day around 4:30 p.m. I was timing our flight and when we got to a little more than halfway to our destination, I said, "Tell me when we get to the place where you think we had our problem yesterday." He said, "It was about right here." The weather was pretty and clear, and we could see everything. I looked all around, and there were big peaks everywhere. I don't know how we got down to 11,500 feet without hitting one of them because there was no way he could have known where they were, as there had been no visibility. It was really rugged country with absolutely no place to have tried to make a crash landing. It was just God.

We got an especially loving welcome from the folks in Cochabamba; I even got kisses from some of the ladies!

Anne asked me why the Lord spared us, but I couldn't come up with any answers, except that Psalm 67 kept coming to mind which teaches that God blesses us not for our selfish ends, but that we may in turn be a blessing to others, and that's what I want the rest of my life to be used for. It is amazing how many of the same thoughts Anne had during those four or five minutes or whatever it was. One thought that comforted her was, "My hope is built on nothing less than Jesus' blood and righteousness."

Now God promised Hezekiah 15 more years of life. I don't think I'm Hezekiah, but so far, God has given me another 25 years and maybe he's going to give me another 10 or 15, but I'm ready to go.

Hostages

*Lots of missionaries have a "hostage" story to tell.
Here's the best one we can come up with for ourselves.*

Anne and I finished our work with the Sirionó people of Bolivia in 1985. During the couple of years before that, we had tried to prepare the people for our leaving.

As time drew near, and as they saw we were serious about moving on to another language group, they expressed disappointment that we would even think of abandoning them.

One day the three big chiefs came to see us, and by their formality and demeanor, I knew it was more than just a friendly visit.

They said, "You keep telling us you are leaving us in a few months. You are our missionaries, and we have not released you. We have decided you should stay with us four more years, then you'll be released."

I was upset. Was it they, rather than Anne and I, and the Lord, who should make such decisions? But I did keep my cool (I think).

I told them that the happiest years of our lives were spent with them. Our four kids were raised there. We could happily spend the rest of our lives there. "But you don't need missionaries now. You have God's Word, men who can preach and teach the Word. You have hymnbooks, primer books, and Bible storybooks. The children, young people, and many adults can now read. You have a bilingual school, teachers for the children, health promoters, trained community leaders. With your help, the things God brought us here for, have been accomplished."

We talked more, but there was no meeting of the minds.

A few days later they returned; they wanted the name of my boss "en los Estados Unidos." "We are writing him a letter, and he will order you to stay four more years, then you'll be released."

This time I reminded them that there are 3,000 other language groups in the world without God's Word in a language they can understand. "We feel God calling us to move on to one of those groups, to give them God's Word in their own language. And if we wait four more years, we'll be too old to do it."

Again there was no agreement. They left.

A few days later, I'm sure after talking it over with many others, they returned to report:

"We are releasing you. In fact, we are sending you to another language group. Go, and do for them what you have done for us. Translate the Word, train preachers and teachers and community leaders. You will be our missionaries to the place where God leads you. We will pray for you and your work. You are free to go."

When the time arrived, they sent us away with a big public function—food, fun, fellowship, fanfare, festivities, speeches, and a reminder that we are their missionaries sent to another language group.

Then they presented us with a handwritten document, signed by many of the Sirionó leaders and others, expressing their appreciation and sending us off as their missionaries "to do for others what you've done for us."

The people declared June 13, 1985 as a day of fiesta in honor of Anne and me. They prepared meat in several big mud ovens around the village, and each family brought a pot of food, such as soup or rice. About 200 Sirionó plus some people from the "outside" world participated in the "fiesta." There were eloquent speeches in Sirionó, and some—by the school supervisor for the area and the *Corregidor* ("county sheriff")—in Spanish. An official document of thanks, written in both Sirionó and Spanish and containing over 75 signatures representing the Sirionó people, was presented to us. We will always cherish this beautiful certificate and the love and gratitude it expresses, even more so since the Sirionó, before knowing Christ, did not know what it was to say "thank you." Over the succeeding years this certificate has brought back many memories of the big part of our lives spent with the Sirionó people. Here is a translation of part of it:

"Señor Perry Priest and wife, our much-loved friends:

God has caused you to stay for a long time here, for the purpose of continually making us understand. We are very happy with you, as you are our teachers. We thank you, Tall-One and wife, for your great love for our Sirionó race. You have constantly made God's Word clear to the Sirionó people, first to those in San Pedro, then to us in Ibiato, as well as to others. You wrote the New Testament for us, translating it to be our very own. We also say thanks very much to Señora Ana, a wonderful nurse to us. You were always thinking of our children as well. You always gave books so they could have school, so our children could learn. We appreciate you very much, our missionary Perry Priest and wife Ana. We thank God for the years you lived in Bolivia teaching us and other indigenous language groups the Gospel of Salvation."

Finishing in Bolivia

Our main assignment in Bolivia was Bible translation, evangelism, and discipleship among the Sirionó people. I also did language surveys, was a translation consultant to other language projects, and served as field director for seven years. Our translation assistant, Chiro, became the first Sirionó pastor. We (mostly Anne) trained several men as bilingual schoolteachers, and they are still teaching 30 years later. In 1972 they were recognized by the government as full teachers and received the same salary as normal school graduates.

The work consisted of language analysis, academic articles, production of primers, hymnals, easy reading materials, and translation of the New Testament and parts of the Old Testament. The contract between our mission and the Bolivian government read, "translation of literature of a high moral value, such as the Bible."

The Sirionó New Testament was published and dedicated in 1977.

Our three boys, Bob, Daniel, and Joel, were born in Bolivia, and Lorna was a USA furlough baby.

All of our mission's work in minority languages in Bolivia was finished in 1985, and Tumi Chucua was given to the government to be used as a normal school. All our missionaries were then assigned to work in other countries. The Bolivia government conferred on our mission the "Condor of the Andes," the highest honor that can be given to a non-Bolivian organization. I had the privilege of accepting the conferral on behalf of the more than 100 Wycliffe workers who had served in Bolivia.

Return to Bolivia

A year after we left Bolivia, Anne and I were asked to go back to Bolivia for a couple of months to visit and encourage the people in eleven of the language groups. Since the two mission airplanes had already been sent to other countries, we had to travel to the different areas by various means, including canoe, motorcycle, truck, and foot. We slept on bamboo beds, in hammocks, on cowhides, or whatever the people were able to provide.

Over and over again we heard, "You *didn't* forget us after all." Every day brought many opportunities to teach and counsel, as well as to listen, sympathize, and love. Some had suffered persecution, severe illness, and flooding. In many places we saw the translated Word of God in use by a growing group of believers who were encouraging each other and reaching out to others. There were disappointments (falling away, immorality, indifference), but there was a strong witness for Christ in every town and village we visited.

When the Cavineña people in the village of La Francia heard that we wanted to visit them, they radioed us to bring a notary public. We arranged for a notary to go with us, but we had no idea as to why they needed him. A crowd of people came out to welcome us. We soon learned why they wanted a notary. They had received their copies of the New Testament in their own language just a year before, and in it they came to understand that God wanted couples to be legally married, not just living together.

So, that same day, nearly every adult of the village was legally married by the notary. For the ceremony they brought out a small homemade table and chairs. The notary sat behind the table, and each couple, or couple-to-be, took their turn at each end of the table. For each couple the notary filled out all the papers, had witnesses to sign, and then admonished each couple to love each other, stick with each other, and be faithful. Then in turn he declared each couple husband and wife. We took pictures of the newlyweds, including their children and in some cases their grandchildren. That night we had a wedding feast of rice, beans, palm heart, and maybe half the roosters of the village.

The following quotes represent the kinds of encouraging statements we heard all summer long:

- From an old man, patriarch of a large family: "Your missionaries taught us how to live."
- From an Ignaciano young man: "There are now so many believers in our village we won't all fit into the church, so we're building a bigger meeting place."
- From a Guarayu man: "I used to be up and down in my Christian life. The reason I'm now strengthened in the Lord is that we now have His Word in our language."
- From a Pacahuara man: "Coni (from a neighboring Chacobo village) teaches us."
- From a Chiquitano Christian leader who runs a very effective health post for his people: "I began my medical training in your living room with nurse Juana as my teacher."
- From Carlos, who studied in our leadership training course and radio repair course: "I was offered (by the cocaine king of Bolivia) a good job with lots of money, but I told him, 'That's not for me!'"
- From an old Sirionó man: "We're so glad Edgar and other young people come out into the fields (where many of the older people live) to teach us God's Word."
- From Estevan: "The priest came to our village and asked all those who 'follow the Gospel' to raise their hands. There are seven Christian families but only six had courage to declare themselves. He threatened us, insulted us, told us he no longer considers us real people, and said we could no longer go to the area hospital for medicines when we are sick. For about a week we were so sad we were like dead people. Then all at once we realized 'God has considered us worthy to suffer for Jesus! It is a privilege!'"
- From an Ese Ejja lady who's been a believer for several years: "God has answered my prayers! My husband has been following Jesus for almost a year now."
- From an 83-year-old pharmacist in Riberalta: "For many years my pharmacy was my life. Now it's just a way to provide contact with people so I can tell them that Jesus died for their sins."
- From a Cavineña rubber gatherer as he showed us his 50-pound ball of rubber: "This ball belongs to the Lord. It is my tithe."

One item of deep concern was that there were several leftist groups in Bolivia seeking to "organize" the indigenous communities. The Christians who go along with them tend to lose their zeal for the Lord. These organizations sponsored a conference to decide on what they hoped to be a "unified alphabet" for all of the Guarani languages. When Carmelo, a Guarayu Christian, returned from the preliminary meetings, he told the believers, "The alphabet of our language will be changed, so we should just put aside our New Testaments." One of these organizations also offered Carmelo a good job and house in the city. He quit going to church and seemed genuinely confused. While we were there he was able to make a new commitment to the Lord and to the believers of his village. Some of the Guarani Christian leaders had hoped that Anne and I could attend the conference. But our suggestion was that they themselves defend the alphabet used in the Guarani and Guarayu Scriptures. Later on we learned that they had very ably and forcefully defended the alphabet, and that the conference did not recommend any changes in any of the languages!

Anne and I agreed that it was the most unusual and interesting summer we'd ever had—maybe even the most enjoyable.

But the trip to the last of the eleven indigenous communities was anything but enjoyable. We surely didn't expect to make an emergency landing at a cocaine factory in the middle of the rainforest!

Just two weeks before, the USA government had pressured the Bolivian government into inviting a large group of American narcotic agents to go to Bolivia (with airplanes and other equipment) to help find all the cocaine processing plants and get rid of them. There was a huge outcry from the Bolivian public. "Why should Americans come to Bolivia to destroy our one crop that is lucrative? Let them try to control cocaine use in their own country, but stay away from Bolivia."

Since our mission planes were no longer in Bolivia, we had to charter a small plane from another mission to take us from the Chiquitano area to Urubicha, a Guarayu village. The missionary pilot was new to Bolivia and to flying over the vast rainforest. So he got lost!

A few minutes after we should have arrived at Urubicha, he said, "We must have overshot our destination!" For almost an hour we had flown over solid virgin rainforest, not an opening nor house to be seen. He became agitated, didn't seem to know what to do. I knew the area somewhat, so suggested he veer to the west, where he could find the Rio Blanco and follow it back to Urubicha. But he wasn't about to listen to a non-pilot, so he kept going.

He said, "We'll go on for five minutes, then turn around and go back to where we started from."

A moment later, we saw in the distance a white plane sitting at the end of a small airstrip that had recently been hacked out of the rainforest. He said, "Look at that missionary airplane. We'll land there and get directions." I told him it was probably a cocaine plane and a cocaine-processing factory.

He said, "But we are almost out of fuel; we have to land!"

I offered to do the talking since he didn't speak much Spanish.

As we landed and taxied to a stop, six men, grimfaced, some with guns, stood beside the plane, three on each side, and they certainly didn't have a welcome sign out.

I opened the window, greeted them, told them we were missionaries, we were lost and needed directions to Urubicha. Then I said, "I think we aren't too far from the Rio Blanco. My wife and I used to live on that river many years ago."

When I said that, the man who was the owner of that place, as well as the pilot of the little white plane, smiled and said excitedly, "Oh, then you are don Perry. My father is Reinaldo _____. When I was a kid, I'd go with him to visit you; I know you. Get out; come in. This is your house. Let us give you some refreshments." We had agreed that we shouldn't get out; we didn't want to see anything. So we told him, "We need to get to Urubicha right away. Just tell this pilot the heading and distance, please." He wouldn't tell us until we had taken some refreshment, so we sat in the plane in the hot sun, baking and sweating, until they brought drinks.

Then he said, "You overshot Urubicha. Take heading so and so, and you'll arrive there in 29 minutes. Vaya con Dios." He was right.

I'm sorta glad Reinaldo's son was at the cocaine factory that day, and I hope he knows I never told on him.

Moving on to Nigeria

In 1987 we went to Nigeria, on loan by Wycliffe Bible Translators to the Nigeria Bible Translation Trust (NBTT). It was a different, but good learning experience to be under a totally African administration. We worked with the Jibu people group and language the twelve years we were there. Our first language assistant, a Muslim, accepted Christ and seemed to be growing in Christ, and even witnessing for Christ. But social and family pressures and threats finally turned him away. Another language assistant, Salamu Mazadu, became a strong believer. His story is written up elsewhere in this book.

At first there wasn't much interest, and most of the village people were afraid of us. We got over that hurdle, but still there was

Perry and Anne in Nigerian dress

little interest in having God's Word translated into their language. I had typhoid, and both of us had many bouts of malaria. And we, especially I, were having trouble learning that tonal language. Why was it so hard to learn? Even four-year-olds could speak it! Had God really led us there? Would we ever be able to translate the Word and see a growing body of believers there? I thought of quitting. But each time I wanted to throw in the towel, I'd think of those who prayed for us, including the Sirionó people in Bolivia who commissioned us to go and do for another people group what we had done for them. That helped to keep me on course until we were able to give the Jibu people the New Testament in their language.

We count it a privilege that the Lord called us and sent us out as His ambassadors to Nigeria.

Meeting a Chief

Some of the Jibu Christians took us to visit the two paramount chiefs and several village chiefs. Their purpose was to introduce us, explain the proposed Bible translation project, and get us accepted into the area. Although all the chiefs were Muslim, they promised us protection and moral support.

There are certain rituals you go through to have an audience with a chief. Here's how it went at one place. Everyone took their shoes off in the courtyard. Then we were ushered into a very elaborate room, where the chief sat in front, on a big purple couch (his throne?). Anne and I were seated on his right in chairs; all his attendants and the people who had gone with us sat on the floor to his left. The Jibu Christians explained the Bible translation project to him, and he said we were welcome in his area and that he would protect us. (He also told us that he had seven wives, over 50 children, and 20 grandchildren! That was 22 years ago, and his family has more than doubled by now!)

High Tone, Low Tone...

Jibu is a tonal language. Every syllable has a tone, either high tone, mid tone, or low tone. High tone is written with an accent mark (ó) over the syllable. Low tone is written with a reverse accent mark (ò) over the syllable. Any syllable without one of these two tone marks, should be pronounced as mid tone. The Jibu caught onto this writing system fast. It was the "red man" (yes, to the Jibu we were red, not white) and his wife who struggled greatly to pronounce the proper tone.

Each of the groups of Jibu words below are spelled exactly alike *except* for the tone marks.

ayír = sandfly   kán = acacia tree
ayir = rib   kan = bracelet
àyir = bush fowl   kàn = vervet monkey

shúnn = maternal uncle íri = only
shùnn = mud fish   írì = species

sún = moon   jau = play
sun = ear   jàu = friend

swánn = load   káb = finish
swann = carry   kab = dig
swànn = burn   kàb = small hut

ji = to eat   gbág = barren
jì = to bury   gbag = dirty pot

Can you imagine the consequences of some of our mistakes?

Language Bloopers

In our language learning, both of us made many mistakes, some embarrassing and some really funny. Anne considered me to be the linguist of the family, and she had wondered whether she'd be able to learn an African language. But the fact is that she did exceptionally well and word got out that the "red man" didn't understand as much Jibu as his wife. One day a man came to ask a favor and he said, "I want to talk to your wife; she can understand better than you."

A man came and told us his daughter was very sick. I said *itau* "I'm glad" instead of *atau* "I'm sorry." Anne was cutting my hair one day when a neighbor came to visit; we wanted to ask if she cuts her husband's hair. Well, we got hair (*jinn*) and head (*shinn*) mixed up, so we asked if she cut her husband's head off. Did she laugh! She even drew her finger across her neck just like we might do.

One night a man was telling us that nearly all his relatives have several wives. Anne very piously said, or thought she said, "I'm glad my husband wants only one wife." What she really said was "I'm glad my husband wants one more wife." We wondered how many rumors got started from that!

There's no word in the Jibu language for the verb "to suffer." Instead, the natural way to say it in Jibu is "to drink suffering." We had fun once when Anne confused the words *shin* (beer/ homebrew) and *shwin* (suffering). A young man told her that the Jibu people drink too much *shin* (homebrew) but she thought he'd said *shwin* (suffering). Anne wanted to say, "If God sends suffering into our lives, we should be willing to drink it." Actually she was saying, "If God sends homebrew into our lives, we should drink it."

His reply, "I can't believe you'd tell us to drink it." The argument continued, he thinking Anne was defending drinking, and she thinking he had fallen into the "Prosperity Gospel" and felt Christians shouldn't ever suffer.

I was in another room about to bust a gut laughing as they talked past each other. Finally I asked, "Are you talking about *shin* or *shwin*?" We had a good laugh, and Salamu (our main translator) went out and told the people, tongue-in-cheek, that the missionary's wife had said that if God provides beer, the people should drink it.

god-house

We tried to visit as many of the eighty-plus Jibu villages as often as we could, making friends and leaving bits of God's Word whenever possible—in greater detail as we learned more of their culture and language.

As we visited the village of Ibango, the chief and some others were building a grass wall around a small hut, so I pitched in and helped as we talked. I even learned to weave the leaves in the way they do it. After a time the young man who had accompanied us and was by then a Christian, came over and, in a low voice, said, "Is it good for a Jesus person to help build an altar?" WOW!! What I thought was to be a toilet turned out to be a pagan god-house.

In spite of all our cultural blunders, we could see the Holy Spirit working in many of the villages.

Now, several years later, there is a nice group of Christians in Ibango. And instead of a god-house, they now have a God house (capital G), a place to worship the true God.

Secret Religion

In the early stage of our learning the Jibu language, we used a cassette recorder often. We would ask people to tell on the recorder a story or an event in their lives or how to plant guinea corn or yams. Then our language assistant, Akyale, would explain it and help us transcribe it, and then we'd translate it into English.

A man from a distant village visited us and asked to talk on our machine. We gave him the microphone but didn't expect anything too significant. And at first, what he said seemed like harmless advice, given not to us but to the Jibu people who might hear it. He said they were to help us, be peaceful and cooperative up to a point. But he used many figures of speech which we didn't understand and which we later realized he didn't want us to understand. He said the people could tell us about the tree, but should not expose the roots. They could show us their upper bodies, but not remove their trousers in our presence. They could teach us but not take us into the bush; not show us their sleeping house. As we later learned, he was one of the leaders in the Jibu traditional religion, and his whole speech was a warning, given in highly figurative language, that nobody should teach us the Jibu secret religion of ancestor worship, idol worship, reincarnation, and blood sacrifices. In language that we wouldn't have understood if our friends hadn't explained it, he was saying that anyone who tells us of their religion would have a curse put on him from which he can never recover; he would deserve whatever happened to him.

People-eaters

A person who is suspected of putting a curse/hex on someone is called a people-eater. In other languages he might be called a witch. The belief is that there is only one way to remove the curse—go to the one suspected of putting on the curse and plead with him and/or pay him in money or farm produce to remove the curse.

During our first month among the Jibu we heard that a man, the brother of our friend, had been eaten by a people-eater. Later we heard that he had been killed in a truck accident. I naively said, "But I thought he was eaten by a people-eater." The answer was, "Yes, and that's the cause of the accident. He was as good as dead long before the accident." (In other words, the accident was the inevitable result of the curse by the people-eater.)

When Anne and I would visit the village of Agba Kunn, I'd always visit one old man, so the people referred to him as my friend. One day a younger man told me, "I guess you don't know that your friend is a people-eater. He has eaten at least eight people in this village." To "eat" someone seemed at first to be only a metaphor, meaning to kill someone by placing a curse on him/them. Later on it became evident that the metaphor is carried even farther.

Mr. Magaji was a fine man, helpful to many needy people. As far as I know, nobody ever thought of him as a people-eater. But he did often drink *shin* and palm wine in excess. When he was into middle age, his stomach began to swell and he was in terrible pain—cirrhosis of the liver. To the people, his swelling stomach was evidence that he was a people-eater.

Under Jibu ideology a people-eater (witch) may be unaware that he is a witch. But his envy, anger, resentment, or jealousy toward another has the mystical power to inflict sickness and death.

Imagine the grief of a man, not just at the thought of dying, but also at the accusation that he is a people-eater, and the disappointment of the family in finding out that, unbeknownst to them, their husband and father must have brought death to several people.

Beer and Beliefs

Most of the Jibu people are farmers. They raise some maize and cassava, but the most important crop is guinea corn. Guinea corn is used primarily to make the ever-present *shin* or home brew. *Shin* also plays a big role in the Jibu secret religion.

The people customarily have just one meal a day and it is cooked and eaten at night, after dark. But *shin* can be drunk throughout the day. It is sour, but even babies are trained to like it. When the baby is only days old, the mother repeatedly puts her finger in the beer and then in the baby's mouth. Soon it begins to enjoy the taste, and by the time the baby is a few months old, it drinks the beer from a cup or gourd.

People go early in the morning to their farms. They take a gourd or other container full of guinea corn beer. During working hours they drink it only when hungry or thirsty, and since the alcohol content is low, it is not sufficient to make them intoxicated. But when they return home in the afternoon, several groups of people may get together at various homes for drinking, and then they are likely to get loud and tipsy. The men and women usually gather in separate homes for this late afternoon drinking.

Shin plays an important role in Jibu communal life. They love work parties, whether it be building a house, preparing the ground for planting, or harvesting the crop. On one day, one man will be owner of the workday. That is, it is his house or farm where a large crew of people work. The next day the work will be done for another person or family. The owner of the workday always provides plenty of *shin*, but it is drunk sparingly (only when hungry or thirsty). Nobody would ever sponsor a work party, or attend, if there's not plenty of *shin* for the whole day. Once a man did call a workday, but the *shin* was watered down. This is not as nourishing, and he was the butt of jokes and criticism.

Men and women have slightly different religious practices, and never practice their native religion together. The men go up on the highest hills, where they kill chickens as blood offerings to their fetishes, and pour *shin* on the ground in worship.

For a long time I considered asking for permission to go with them to observe, so as to better understand their religion. Finally I asked several of the men if I could accompany them. They indicated it would be acceptable. They were to let me know when they would go. But they always went without informing me. So I got the message that they didn't really want me to go. Maybe the Lord also didn't want me to go, who knows?

When the men do their religious rites in the village, the women must never be present. The belief is that if women do watch it, even from afar, they will become crazy. So they and the children stay in their homes the entire time. The women have their own religious practices and rites, but at a different time.

The Jibu religion is a very secret religion. On many occasions, as I learned more of the language, I was able, without attacking their religion, to explain the Word of God to many, and tell them that Jesus' message is true, and is so important that He commanded us to tell it to people all over the world. They understood the contrast.

Roadblock

In Nigeria, when we'd drive from Serti (the Jibu town we lived in) to Jos (the city headquarters for Nigeria Bible Translation Trust), about 450 miles over some bad roads, we'd usually get up at 3:30 a.m., hop in the already packed car, and start off, hoping to get to Jos by nighttime. On one occasion, the alarm clock didn't go off, so we slept late and didn't get off until after 5:00 a.m. I was upset, and ready to smash that clock. About an hour later, just at daybreak, we came to a bridge that had big stones across it to stop the traffic. We thought of armed robbers, but there were none. The boulders were too big for me to move, so we went back a mile or so and found a man willing to help me.

After moving the stones we continued our journey, and at the next village there were two big trucks full of passengers. They stopped us and asked if we had been robbed, and asked, "How did you get across the bridge?" They told us one truck had been stopped at the bridge before daybreak by armed robbers. All their money, watches, and other valuables had been taken, and one man had been wounded. The robbers made them return without crossing the bridge, so they had warned the second truck which had been following.

We were told that these robbers stop night travelers, and then flee into the bush just at daylight.

The alarm clock served us well for several years after that. Maybe it knew something that night that we hadn't known.

Tackling Malaria and Typhoid

Don't ever try to tackle malaria and typhoid fever at the same time.
They'll get the best of you!

It all started Friday, March 18, 1988. I got sick while studying with Akyale and had to lie down. I got gradually worse over the next three days with high fever, headache, and body aches. On Sunday Anne went over to the military post to see Dr. Iko Yoba, a friend of ours. He had just returned from a six-week absence. Dr. Yoba began to treat me for malaria and typhoid. That afternoon was so hot Anne moved me out under the mango tree, because I was sweating badly and had a high temperature. She kept washing me in cold water and the Jibu people took turns fanning me, two at a time, for over five hours a day.

Tuesday (Day 5) a mission airplane was scheduled to come at 7:30 a.m. so Anne went to the radio and talked to the pilot. He said he'd come back in the afternoon and take us to Takum where there was a little hospital. He even had a pallet for me to lie on. That was the first time in 34 years of missionary aviation I ever traveled lying down. (I was to repeat it four days later). I was put on IV drip at the Takum hospital and given many kinds of medication. The doctor thought it was malaria, but fortunately he kept up the typhoid treatment. I had fever off and on all the time and Anne was kept busy sponging me off and fanning me. One night she had to do that from midnight to daylight. The hospital didn't provide food or drinking water. The missionaries there were very kind to us and brought food and water, but I didn't eat much. One day Anne asked me what I thought I could eat. I said jello was all I could think of. Without knowing what I had requested, the doctor brought me a dish of mango jello that afternoon! I could only eat a little of it.

After four days and many pints of IV drip, the doctor said I should be taken to the Jos hospital where they had better lab facilities as I was weaker and no better. This was Saturday, Day 9. So at 3:30 p.m. after a hard day of work, the pilot flew us to Jos, even though it meant he couldn't get back home that day. The Jos hospital continued the IV drips and the same treatments, and their lab confirmed I had both malaria and typhoid fever, plus amoeba! I began to improve on Day 11. On Day 12 they discontinued the IV drip and I started eating a little; so on Day 13 they let me out of hospital to go to NBTT headquarters for recuperation.

There was a lot to be thankful for. I'm glad both doctors treated me for both sicknesses even though they weren't sure which I had. I'm thankful the plane was available both times we needed it. The missionaries in Takum were super helpful. I don't think I'd have made it without Anne's help—her constant attention, boundless energy, and wise decisions when I was too sick to help with anything.

It's Lumpy

One day Anne told me the cushion she normally sat on seemed to have a lump in it. Next it was the lumpy bed. When I tried the same spots it always felt fine to me. It was a couple of weeks before she realized the lump was a part of her! We immediately went to Jos.

Anne had a large growth, attached to the pelvis, removed from her hip. A highly recommended young surgeon from Dallas, Texas, who was in Jos for nine months to help out in missions, did the surgery. Since the medical facilities in Nigeria were not all that great the biopsy had to be sent to the USA for checking. It turned out that it was not malignant.

At first we were discouraged by the interruption in "our" schedule, but the Lord reminded us that *His* plans are best and will be carried out no matter what.

River Blindness

We would often make trips to various Jibu villages. It was heartbreaking to see a blind person in almost every home in the villages nearer the river. River blindness is caused by the bites of a small, hump-backed fly known as the "black fly." Worms are injected into a person by the fly, and eventually the worms affect the eyes as well as other parts of the body. First there may be redness and tears, then the cornea becomes scarred, and finally sight is lost. There had never been a good medicine for river blindness without dangerous side effects. In 1988 we were overjoyed to hear on the Voice of America radio news program that Merck Pharmaceuticals had a new, simple, very effective medicine (with few side effects) which prevents river blindness even in people who are already infected and having initial symptoms. Merck offered the medicine for free to African countries who would promise to distribute it and keep accurate records.

It took about three years of writing letters to the Ministry of Health, the World Health Organization, Merck Pharmaceuticals, and our governor—to try to get the new river blindness drug Ivermectin for our area. Finally, our county was chosen as one of three counties to begin a pilot program with the drug. Two young men went all over our county by motorcycle—handing out the medicine, treating about 16,000 people. Shortly afterward, we received the Ivermectin that we personally had ordered (over a year previously) and we were able to do the mop-up operation—giving it to people that for one reason or another didn't get it from the fellows on the motorcycle. One Sunday we went to a village that was completely skipped and treated about 200 people there. We were able to have a church service there as well.

We were happy that we could help meet physical as well as spiritual needs of the people. The physical blindness seemed to be a little picture of the terrible spiritual blindness we saw all around us, with the Word of God as the only remedy.

Big Bertha

This is the saga of the tryst between Bertha and me.
Bertha is the biggest thing I've caught since 1956
when Anne fell for my line.

Bob and Willie (missionaries working in Jos with the SIM mission) pulled up in Serti on a Wednesday in March 1992, on their way to camp out at the fishing hole. They invited me to go with them, but I didn't accept. The next afternoon as we finished our work, Anne said, "I think you should go to the river and at least spend one night with them. They really wanted you to go with them." I told her I never have any luck and I was too tired. But Akyale was still there and she got him on her side, as he was always ready to go fishing, so I was pushed out of my own house and sent to the river. Guess that proves I'm not a real fisherman who'd never have to be urged. We (Akyale and I) got to their campsite just as they were sitting down to an early supper, so the two pieces of pie Anne sent for them didn't last long.

Then the four of us hiked to the fishing place about an hour up-river. We got there maybe 45 minutes before dark. I taught Akyale how to cast with my small rod and reel and we fished awhile. Then around 6 p.m. we had a heavy rain—the first in nearly five months.

Meanwhile, back at the ranch, Anne was asking the Lord to forgive her for sending her favorite husband out on a night like that. She could see that the rain was coming even as she prayed it would not rain.

The rain soaked all four of us thoroughly, and I wished we were at home. At 7 p.m. it stopped for awhile so we began fishing again. Akyale got a strike and the 15-pound test line immediately broke and the lure was lost, of course. I said, "I'll put another lure on for you, but let me cast a couple of times first." It was at that very moment I met Bertha. She tried to pull me into the river. I thought I'd hooked a hippo. She went up the river, down the river, did two or three jumps out of the water like Flipper. It was dark but a Niger perch is almost white so we could see her when she jumped. Well, she and I both did what we could at our respective ends of that 30-pound test line. (I had tried to use 40-pound test line on two previous trips, but found out you can't cast as far with heavy line, so I decided to put 30-pound test line on, thinking I'd never catch anything that would challenge that.) I kept reeling her in and she kept pulling the line back out. The fellows wanted to relieve me and finally one of them (I was too excited to remember which one it was) took the pole for a couple of minutes, but I didn't want another kid playing with my toy so I took it right back. Finally Bertha sort of gave up and I reeled her to the edge and Bob, with his long gaff, hooked her and we got her up on the rocks.

They were as happy as I, and as for Akyale, he was ecstatic as this was the biggest fish he'd ever seen and the first he had ever seen caught with a lure. We had fun estimating her weight. Our guesses ran from 70 to 115 pounds. We cut a pole, put it through her mouth and jaw, and started back to camp as it was again raining. With the pole on the shoulders of two of us the tail touched the ground.

It was dark, raining, no moon or stars, and we couldn't find the trail so we wandered around in the bush with that fish on our shoulders, each thinking the trail was in a different direction. Well, we all took our turns carrying Bertha and I was so tired I wanted to throw her away, but nobody would agree. I think Bob and Willie saw her as their ticket to another fishing trip the next year as their wives had told them if they came home without fish, this might be their last trip (actually they had each caught a smaller one the day before).

We finally found our trail and got back to camp a little after 10:00 p.m. I had wanted to come on home that night and cut up the fish and give it away before it spoiled, but by this time the road was soaked and impassable. The fellows had brought four ice chests full of ice (they really came well equipped with everything—lanterns, table, tent, ice, scales, beds, and gaffs, and the only thing I had was the soggy clothes on my back and the mandate from Anne to get a fish). We had to cut poor Bertha into three pieces to weigh her as Willie's scales weighed only up to 50 pounds. She weighed 102 pounds. We packed her in ice for the night.

Akyale and I spent the night in the car (I didn't say slept). The next morning the road was a bit drier so we went on home. Pieces of Bertha went to Christians, Muslims, and pagans. We shared with another missionary, his Nigerian in-laws, our workers, the workers at the clinic, lots of friends and one enemy, the blind, the snake-bitten, and the sick. Bertha found her way inside at least 100 people, I'd guess. Bob and Willie got four big hunks to take home.

That night, after we had finished supper, Bob and Willie came to our house to spend the night. Anne cooked them fish and hushpuppies. Willie is German and had never heard of hushpuppies.

So ended the life of a great lady (I named her Bertha instead of Bert when we found eggs inside her), and so ends this tale.

By the way, Bertha may have set an all-time record as being the biggest fish in the whole wide world ever to have been caught in our little river. However, they say Niger perch grow to 200 pounds or more in the bigger rivers like Niger and Benue.

Locked Out

It was midafternoon when Anne and I arrived at the small village of Agba Kunn. Most of the people were in the drinking house, having just returned, tired and thirsty, from their farms. We visited, then read and explained Scripture to them and played some Gospel tapes. Anne chose Titi, a young man who seemed bright and alert, and taught him how to use a hand-cranked tape player. We left the tape player and some Gospel tapes in his language with Titi, and he agreed to play the tapes from time to time for the whole village. Nobody in the village could read, and nobody was a Christian. Soon it looked like rain and it was almost dark, so we hurried to the car, parked outside the village, to drive the 35 miles back home, only to discover I had locked the keys in the car! Just at that moment the downpour started. What do we do? We're sopping wet, it's raining harder and harder, and half the village is standing in the rain waiting to tell us goodbye. Finally, in desperation, we decided to break one of the small windows—I hit it with a rock; it wouldn't break. I got a bigger rock, but that glass was like steel, and I was guessing the people thought I was crazy to beat on the car like that. Finally I gave up and we all went back to the village and crawled under the low roof of a kitchen to get out of the rain. I asked about tools. Nobody had a hammer. The only tool in the whole village was a small screwdriver. With that, we finally got the window broken, and in the dark we made it to home-sweet-home and to dry clothes by 8:30.

Titi played the tapes many, many times for the village people, and he soon put his trust in Jesus and wanted more instruction. We kept up with him, and he learned to read and went to a five-year Bible school. Then he went to distant villages as an evangelist. He has started churches in at least two villages and continues to serve the Lord. We pray for him and other village evangelists all over the world.

Not to worry about the car window. We got the glass replaced for $6, as there is basically one kind of car in Nigeria, and there are plenty of wrecked Peugeots for used parts.

Holding Hands

It was the first year for us in Nigeria. A neighbor, Ayuba, came and invited me to go with him to a soccer match a mile or so down the road. I agreed. As soon as we started out, he took my hand. I felt a bit uncomfortable with that. Each time we met someone on the way, I'd take my hand out of his, and shake hands with the person. But then Ayuba would immediately take my hand again. I knew that in their culture, holding hands was nothing more than showing friendship or camaraderie. But I was a creature of another culture. I felt more and more uncomfortable. I thought, "What if my mother could see me now?" I almost felt guilty. I purposely got lost from him at the soccer match. What a relief! Later on as I got more into the Jibu culture, I could more easily let a boy or man hold my hand, knowing that he wanted only to be my friend.

I did wish that Anne would hold hands with me more, just to show Jibu husbands and wives one way to express their love. I've never seen a Nigerian husband and wife hold hands. Husbands and wives hardly ever touch in public, and hardly speak to each other when they are with other people. Many men, even Christians, seemed to feel superior to their wives. Wives, daughters, and young children normally eat in the cookhouse. Men and their friends and older boys eat together in a more visible place. I felt it was the result of Muslim and pagan influence, so I liked to walk down the road holding Anne's hand and enjoying conversation. But I guess I was a failure, as nobody followed my example in that!

Runaway Bride

Traditionally, weddings among the Jibu people consist mainly of the man getting permission from the parents of the expected bride, agreeing to a bride price or dowry, and the bride being escorted by her friends to the groom's home.

Danjuma was to be married to a girl who lived nearby, and all arrangements had been made with her parents. He asked me to go to her house in the car at sundown and bring her to his house, where he and his friends would be waiting. Her riding in a car would add prestige and flavor to the event.

When I arrived at her house, the people informed me that the bride-to-be had run away. "But don't worry; just wait a few minutes and we'll find her." After an hour, they came and said, "We've caught her; she's on the way." Soon I heard loud crying and bellowing like an animal being taken to the slaughter. As they got closer, I could hear all her friends making merry as they pushed and pulled her along. When they arrived, she stiff-armed the car so as not to enter, but her friends, having a fun time, folded her arms and pushed her in. The whole way to the groom's house, she wailed loudly; her friends enjoying it all.

When we arrived, Danjuma was waiting. The wedding was over.

I learned later that the bride is always to pretend that she does not want to be married, runs away and hides, but always at a place where she can easily be found. It's just a cultural thing, and to do otherwise could be interpreted as lack of love for her parents.

Danjuma and his wife are happily married, and have a growing family and both are following Christ.

Buying a Bride

One Sunday we went for a service to a village where the people had just begun to believe. An old blind man, who played the
drum for the church services, and who had only the old, tattered
clothes on his back, excitedly told us that a woman had promised
to marry him if he could provide her with a dress. So later, when
we passed by his village, Anne took him a few pieces of women's
clothing. You never saw a blind man hurry down the path as fast
as that fellow did when he heard we had returned! He showed
the clothes to all who were there, and in true Jibu fashion, everyone thanked us profusely. We hope that by now he has acquired
his new wife!

Jibu Funeral

One Sunday we took one of the evangelists that we had been train-ing and went to a village to have a service. When we arrived, the village chief told us he felt we wouldn't be able to "talk God's Word" that day, as a woman had died just an hour or so before. Many of the men were already digging the grave. I went over to help a bit. According to custom, they buried the corpse as soon as the grave was ready.

After the grave was covered, they took an earthen pot about the size of a person's head, made a hole in the bottom of it and turned it upside down on the grave, leaving the upper half uncovered. (This hole represents a person's fontanel. When they next see, on a newborn baby, this soft spot pulsating, they will "know" the deceased person has been reincarnated in this baby.) After that, a calabash dish was chopped up and all the pieces spread over the grave. Thus they were putting a curse on anyone who might still hold a grudge against the deceased, or isn't friendly and helpful to the remaining family members. "They won't last any longer than the calabash did," they say.

All the men who had helped in the burial then went over to where several large containers of water had been brought for the ceremonial washing. They washed their hands, arms, faces, all their upper bodies, and then their feet. This is to prevent "Death" from going home with them.

Next we went to the place where all the women were wait-ing. (It is taboo for a woman to attend a burial.) The village chief then said to all the men, "Everyone now sit down for the thank-you." An elderly lady, representing all the women who had been waiting, then came out of the cookhouse. She very ceremoniously prostrated herself on the ground in front of all of us men, and on behalf of all the women, she thanked us over and over again for being willing to bury the lady (a dangerous job if all the rituals are not closely followed). With her elbows on the ground, she clapped her hands during the whole speech, in which she wished blessing and protection for all who had helped.

Prayer Letters

Normally, our prayer letters were printed and mailed in the USA. Every two years or so, Anne and I would mail one issue of our prayer letter directly from the field, just to be able to write personal notes on some of them and let people receive something directly from overseas with Bolivian or Nigerian stamps.

On those occasions, we would address and stamp the envelopes ahead of time, and put into each envelope any correspondence we had received from that person over the past year to make it easy to reply to each letter.

One time, when we were in Nigeria, I suggested we write at least one sentence to each recipient, whether or not there was a letter from them. Anne was afraid it would take too much time away from the work to write 200 or 300 notes. I told her I could write notes on at least 100 prayer letters in one day. She bet I couldn't, but I determined to do it. So one day after the prayer letter was printed, I wrote and wrote, and when I counted one hundred envelopes, I rested. I was proud I had won the bet.

However, a couple of months later, we got a letter from Larry and Jane saying, "Why did you send us an envelope with nothing in it except two old letters we had written you?" So I guess I had written notes on only ninety-nine, which means that Anne won the bet!

A Fable

This was a Christmas story for our grandchildren in 1998.

We dug a garbage hole a few weeks ago and recently I saw that a frog had fallen into it. I knew that he would die in there as there was nothing for him to eat or drink. I wanted to save him, so I lay down on the ground to reach him, but my arm wasn't long enough. Then I got a hoe and told the frog to get on the hoe and I'd save it from certain starvation and death. He wouldn't obey. So I gently slipped the hoe under him and tried to pull him out. He just jumped off. I'd say, "Stay on the hoe and you'll be saved," but each time he'd jump off the hoe. Pretty dumb frog, no?

I never did save him. He's still in the hole, now dead. Was it because he was stubborn? Yes. Was it also because he didn't trust me and didn't understand my language? Yes. If I could have become a frog, jumped into the hole with him, and talked Toad-ese or Sapo-neese[1] to him, I think he would have listened and understood, and be alive today. Well, that is just what Jesus did for us. He became like us, came into our world, talked our human language so we could understand, and told us exactly how to be saved and have abundant life. His name is Immanuel, which means "God with us." His coming into the world and becoming human like us, is called "Incarnation." Spanish *carne* ("flesh") is a close relative of Incarnation. Jesus became carne/flesh for us at the first Christmas, and He understands all about us and is mighty to save!

---

[1] The Spanish word for "toad" is "sapo."

More Translation Treasures

Baby Jesus in a Gourd?

Did you know that the baby Jesus was lying in a "big gourd" when the shepherds went to worship him? Well, not exactly, but we had some fun translating that passage. Hosea, our translation assistant at the time, insisted we render manger as *kwai* (gourd) where animals eat. I insisted it wasn't a gourd, but a kind of box (since they don't have mangers or feed troughs). He said it couldn't be a box, or the baby would have suffocated (to the Jibu, all boxes have lids). I drew him a picture of a manger and he said I had drawn a "gourd," not a box. It turns out that *kwai*, in addition to meaning gourd, also means a feed trough, or any kind of container. This verse was much more understandable translated like he suggested rather than like I had originally wanted it.

Carrying the Sick

One morning a man from a village inside the bush came and asked me to go in the car to get a very sick lady and take her back to Serti for treatment. When we got to the place where the creek is too deep for the car, here they came carrying the lady on a board on their heads. This is the method for carrying the sick and the dead, as well as all other loads. It reminded me of the passage we had checked that week, Luke 7, where Jesus raises the widow's son from death. They were carrying the corpse when Jesus stopped them and told the dead man to stand up. If it is translated literally, Africans get the impression the dead man was told to stand up while he was on the heads of the carriers—probably a little risky. A minor adjustment, like "stand on the ground," which is the implied meaning, will correct this wrong impression.

The Jesus Film in Jibu Language

The New Testament translation into Jibu was finished (1996) and at the printers, so Anne and I could turn to other projects that had been on the to-do list. One was the production of the Jesus film in the Jibu language.

We had talked about the project to the people, and they were eager to help. Twenty-eight people were chosen to speak, one for Mary, one for Simeon, one for John the Baptist, and several for the disciples. Joseph Leman took the part of Jesus, and Salamu Mazadu the narrator role.

The Jibu people had seen a bit of drama, and at first they thought the speakers were to act out their parts. Once we became aware of their misconceptions we explained that they were just to have speaking parts, and the audio would be dubbed into the existing film.

When all was in readiness, Tom and Paulette Garman, vernacular media specialists, came out to Serti to do the recording. We set up a "recording studio" in our bedroom: blankets, sheets, mattress, and grass mats covered most of the walls and ceiling.

It was necessary to have total quietness during the recording sessions. Tom, a perfectionist, wouldn't even let Anne boil water in the kitchen! We had many interruptions—people walking by, people coming into the "studio" to see what was being done, chickens crowing and cackling, motorcycles driving by, and a blind, crazy beggar coming to the window multiple times and refusing to be quiet. Finally the people appointed "policemen" to stay in front of our house to ask passers-by not to talk or make noise. The recording was finished in seven days, and we had a private showing just for those who had a speaking part. They were overjoyed. Joseph, who spoke for Jesus, said, "Now I can die in peace and my voice will continue to tell my people about the Savior."

The voice recordings were sent to the USA to be edited and mixed with the film. When we received the finished product, there was a dedication service, and for the next two dry seasons we showed the film 100 times in various villages, usually in the marketplace or in the center of the village.

At first the women refused to watch the film with the men. They sat on the ground far away from the men and the screen. The women believe that if they see the men practicing their religion, they will go mad or get sick and die. One village chief called me aside and asked if I thought it safe for the women and children to see the film. Chiefs from other villages wondered the same thing, but didn't express it as overtly. I always told them that Jesus never said anything in secret; He said, "In secret I spoke nothing." His good news is for everyone.

In all the villages, the men would sit on the ground near the screen, and the women and children would sit far behind the men. The people had never before seen a film. Some had not even seen a picture in a book. At the first showing in each village, the women were inquisitive, but very afraid. Some watched the film from afar, gradually coming closer, and they would run away when the epileptic boy was shown, fearing that the evil spirit that caused the boy to have a fit might jump out on them. When the camera zoomed in on Jesus' face making it larger and larger, they would run away, saying, "He's coming to get us." But after one or two showings in each village, there was less fear, and some began to believe.

In some villages, when the cock crowed at Peter's betrayal of Jesus, the roosters all over the village would begin crowing. (Like everybody else, roosters like to hear things in their own mother tongue!)

As we went to the villages to show the film some of the new believers would accompany us, and help carry the equipment. They made quite a sight walking down trails carrying the VCR, projector, truck battery (for running the VCR and projector since there was no electricity), and screen on their heads. At first I carried the projector, the most delicate of the equipment. I didn't like seeing that on someone's head. But once I fell down with the projector as we crossed the river, and from that time I decided it was safer on someone else's head than with me. Yes, they can walk for miles with a bottle of kerosene upright on the head, and never spill a drop!

Once while driving to a village, we met Zakariya, one of the newly assigned evangelists, walking along the road. He told us this story. "When you showed the film in Kombotann, you thought there wasn't much interest. But, as a result of their seeing the film, they called me to come to help them, and that's where I've been. Seven men wanted to believe in Christ, so I taught them, then they asked the village chief to choose a plot of land where they could build a hut for worship." He had walked seven miles each way, but he was rejoicing in what the Lord was doing.

Our screen for showing the film was just four boards made into a rectangular frame, and a white sheet was stretched across it, and hung on trees. Once when there were more people than could get to the front side of the screen, some began to go behind the screen to watch. I walked back there, and was surprised to see that the picture was as clear on the back side as on the front of the screen. So from then on, when the crowd was too big, we'd invite some to watch from the other side.

In Nigeria, as well as in other parts of Africa, it is considered very impolite to give someone something by using the left hand. But in the film, Jesus hands out food with the left hand. When the film is viewed from the reverse, however, He is seen as using the proper hand.

On each trip to show the film, various young men who are zealous for the Lord, would take turns accompanying us. After each showing, I or one of them would summarize the Gospel and follow up with teaching. Churches were planted in many villages as a result of the Jesus film.

Jibu New Testament Dedication

The people worked hard for many days to make the dedication service of the Jibu New Testament a success. They appointed several committees, like Feeding, Sleeping, Program, and Security, and a few Muslim men seemed happy to be included on the committees. The men cut forked posts and poles and palm fronds and built four brush arbors in a circle for shade. The women spent many hours preparing food for the people who came from other villages and from Jos. Our good friends, Hon. Dr. Samuel Gani, ex-Deputy Governor of Taraba State (where we lived), and his wife Lois drove over 1400 kilometers to be with us. They added a lot to the atmosphere and prestige of the meeting. About 30 friends from Jos (an 11-hour trip), came to help us celebrate, including a good number of the NBTT staff.

The program went smoothly and lasted only three hours instead of the four or more we expected. There were special numbers from village choirs; speeches in Jibu, Hausa, and English, a sermon in Jibu, and lots of other activities. Mrs. Veronica Gambo, wife of the NBTT director, made a big cake in the form of the open Jibu New Testament. Everyone got a taste of it. I introduced the main translators and literacy workers. Anne gave a brief message and object lesson in Jibu on the importance of reading the Word daily. Rufkatu, a young woman whom Anne taught to read, was responsible for reading one of the Scripture lessons. One teenage boy quoted from memory 1 Corinthians 13 and another quoted Romans 12. They didn't stumble even once. The people liked it, and in true Nigeria fashion many went up to them and put money on their head, letting it fall to the ground. Later, when we started selling the New Testaments, two people bought copies for these two boys. After the service, there was lots of singing and dancing and rejoicing which went on until midnight.

Many people, including a few Muslims, bought New Testaments, and several bought multiple copies to give to those not able to buy. It was encouraging to see their enthusiasm in reading and showing the Book to others. A Muslim man told us, "I went home, locked myself in my room, and read and read and read. The New Testament is very clear and its teaching is good."

One blacksmith, a Muslim, made me a local hoe in exchange for a Jibu New Testament, and later told me he and his son, a high school student, were reading it.

The Jibu wanted us to stay with them longer. All farming in that area of Nigeria is done with a short-handled grub-hoe, so we told them that we had helped them obtain the hoe (Word of God), and now they are the ones to work with it.

Salamu's Story

Shortly after we settled in Serti, Taraba State, Nigeria, we began to visit the surrounding villages to learn about the culture, the people, and the Jibu language. The people along the road were very friendly and talkative. We visited the village of Abadogo, a couple of miles off the road and into the bush. The people there were seemingly afraid of us. They would talk just a bit, then pick up their hoe and go to their farms. There was one boy there, who appeared to be about 12 years old; he was crippled, so we stayed and talked with him. He was dabbing mud on upright sticks to make a mud wall for his sleeping room. He was very alert, and interested in everything we told him. He told us his life story as we helped him daub mud on the wall.

> **Salamu:** "When I was a child my father and mother put me in school. I learned to read in Hausa, but I wondered why they didn't teach me in my own language, Jibu. Later I was able to write some easy words in my own language, but I had no idea how to write most of the words. So I became very sad as I decided God must have created my language so it couldn't be spelled on paper.
>
> "Then I began to have leg pain and couldn't continue school. Everyone convinced my father to take me to another village where the shaman could divine, with turtle shells, who had put a curse on me. While I was there, I received the news that people had killed my father and cut off his head. I was sad beyond words and my leg was worse—infection was in the bone—I wasn't able to go to the burial."

Salamu had never heard of the Bible or Jesus Christ. We told him we wanted to learn his language and translate God's Word into his language. Anne and I told him we wanted to take him to Serti, where there was a health clinic. He had never seen a doctor, but he quickly accepted our offer. He stayed near us during the next few weeks while receiving injections of penicillin each day. He came to our house every day after his injection. We showed him two little books in his language—stories about Jesus' teaching, his miracles, his dying on the cross for our sins. How happy he was to see that God's Word was in his language. He learned very quickly to read in Jibu.

His leg wasn't getting any better so we took him to two other doctors, but there was still no improvement. Finally we took him to the city of Jos, where there were good hospitals.

Thanks to a missionary doctor who specialized in osteomyelitis, Salamu had the surgery he needed. His leg was split open and little pieces of rotting bone were removed. The leg was left open and was scrubbed daily with disinfectant—terribly painful, but necessary. After he was discharged, and while we waited for his leg to continue healing, he stayed with us in an apartment.

To help him pass the time, we set him up with an old upright typewriter and an English typing book. At that point, he did not know any English, but he quickly learned to touch type with all ten fingers. Soon he was able to type business letters in English, letter perfect. Then he began to type in the Jibu language.

When the three of us returned to Serti, we asked him to be our typist for the translation, and Anne taught him to type on the computer. He was elated. We would give him the handwritten translation in Jibu, and he would type it letter perfect, even correcting our spelling and tone marks. Then he began to make changes in the translation, and I warned him not to do that. "But it is better this way," he said. Soon the other translators and I realized that his changes were usually an improvement. Although with scant formal education, he quickly learned Bible translation principles, and did the initial drafts of some of the New Testament alone. He dedicated his life to preach and teach the Word all over Jibu land. He helped some of his age-mates to preach and teach.

At first they would all go together each weekend to a village to witness and teach the Word. Later they went by twos to witness and teach.

Once they told me, "This weekend we are going to Mamjim to witness." I said, "Don't you remember what the village chief there said—that he would prohibit all teaching about Jesus and the Bible in his village?" They said they remembered that, but still wanted to attempt it. So off they went on Friday afternoon. They returned Sunday afternoon saying, "Let us tell you what happened in Mamjim. At first our plan was to enter the village from the back side and witness to as many people as possible before the village chief could throw us out." Any visitor is supposed to go first to the village chief and tell him why he has come. They decided to do it the proper way, although they felt sure he would ask them to leave. They went straight to his house, told him they wanted his permission to spend the weekend there and share God's Word with some of the people. He slapped his hand down and said, "Absolutely not! If you have come here for that, you must leave." There was an older man sitting on the ground with his back to a tree, and he spoke up saying, "These are just boys, and they are our Jibu people. Maybe we should let them stay for two nights." Now in America, we worship youth, but in Africa, older men are respected. So the village chief felt he needed to obey the old man, and he allowed them to stay. The young men went to many homes there and shared the Gospel with the people. They came back rejoicing that God had opened the way for them to share the Word in that village. They told us that many people there were interested in learning more. They said, "We are praying God will open wide the door."

At that point, it was time for us to return to the USA for six months, and we had no idea what would happen in that village. You might never guess where we went to church that first Sunday back in Nigeria. The village of Mamjim! They had continued to go to the village and people had responded to the Gospel. The people there asked the village chief to designate a piece of land so they could build a church, and amazingly, he did so. Several families had accepted Christ, and the village chief quit his threats. The Gospel marches on!

Anne and I, along with the young men, asked God to raise up many followers of Christ in all the villages, and He answered. Each of the men went as evangelists to live for several months in assigned villages, and churches began springing up. Salamu visited them, encouraged them, and prayed for them. He gradually took over part of the work that Anne and I were doing. While I translated, he and Anne would call the young evangelists together for a week to study. Sometimes they had classes in Bible, sometimes in planning sermons, sometimes in doing literacy. The work was moving ahead. Samaila, one of the young men, was musical. He and Anne wrote and taught several praise songs in Jibu music style, and a hymnal was published. Some of the songs got out to far-off villages we had never been to.

As a teenager and then a young man, Salamu spent much time in our home from 1990-1996. He had a gift for making the Scriptures sound natural and clear in the Jibu language. He was a good teacher, a good preacher, and seemed to have a flair for public relations.

We wanted to reward him for his faithfulness in the translation work, so we told him that when the translation was finished, we would help him get training in a profession and help him get started in it. I was thinking of something like blacksmith work or house-building with mud blocks. But toward the end of the translation work, he surprised us by saying he felt he should enter seminary. How could a man who had been to school sporadically for only six years get accepted into seminary? A high school diploma was a requirement. And seminary is taught in English; he hadn't known any English before he came to us. He had never written an essay, never taken a quiz in English.

However, long before this, we had recognized his exceptional intelligence and insatiable desire for knowledge. He had learned English first by listening to Anne and me and asking hundreds of questions, then by learning to read our English Bible, commentaries, exegetical helps, and periodicals.

Salamu

In faith, we helped him apply to the Veenstra Seminary, about 300 miles away. I wrote a cover letter guaranteeing that, if accepted, he would be at the top of his class after a year or two. Well, he traveled to the seminary with his preliminary application filled out; they gave him a Bible test and an English test, and then declared that he knew more Bible and English than most of the applicants. He was accepted, and began his four years of seminary training in 1996. By 1997 he was number one in his class.

Anne and I left Nigeria and returned to the United States in early 1999. We were past retirement age and having many health issues. Although Salamu had not yet graduated from seminary, we, as well as the Jibu committee, saw Salamu as the ideal one to take leadership of the Jibu work, and we left Nigeria in confidence that Salamu would continue on in the work.

One of Salamu's requirements for graduation was to produce and publish a technical article related to the ministry. His was one of the top two papers in his class. The subject was "The Need to Minister the Word of God in the Mother Tongue" (instead of a trade language which is not well understood by the hearers).

Salamu was to graduate in June 2000. Two months before graduation he was involved in a car accident. The driver was killed, others were seriously hurt. Salamu had a broken pelvis plus cuts and bruises on his head and body, and he was unconscious. The injured were taken to a small hospital, but not much was being done for them. When Salamu regained consciousness, he was able to get someone to send a message to NBTT (Nigeria Bible Translation Trust). They immediately sent a vehicle for him, and he was taken to the SIM/ECWA hospital in Jos for two months of treatment and recuperation. Our dear friends at NBTT fed him, washed his clothes, helped with medicine and other expenses, cared for his "toiletries" as he called it, and much, much more. While recuperating flat on his back, he translated into Jibu a little booklet called "Who is God?" While Salamu was still recuperating, the seminary principal and vice-principal went to visit him, and declared him a "graduate of Veenstra Seminary," which meant he did not have to make up the two months he missed!

Salamu had promised the Lord he would not look for a wife, or marry, until he found a young Jibu woman who was fully committed to the Lord. There seemed to be quite a few committed men, but few women. The Muslims in the area have lots more prestige and usually more wealth, so the marriageable-age girls, as well as their parents, prefer a Muslim husband for her.

One time he was in a village counseling a husband and wife. After their time together, he bowed his head and said to the Lord, "Lord, why do you give me such a difficult task, and not provide a wife to help me in the work? This job is way too big for me. I need a wife, please." Soon after this, Salamu heard of a young lady in a distant village who had been proposed to by several Muslim young men. Each time she said, "No, I won't marry anyone who is not a Christian." When Salamu heard about her, he said to himself—sight unseen: "That is my wife!" He went to her village, made her acquaintance, met her parents, and a few months later they were married. He tells us that not only does she help in the ministry, but she also makes good soup!

Salamu went on to become ordained. He is a good preacher, teacher, and organizer. The Jibu Christians consider him to be their leader. He directs and promotes the work of evangelism and church planting in the many (over 80) Jibu villages. Emails and phone calls from him detailing the growth of the Church among the Jibu people bring us great joy.

Comparing Two Countries

There are many interesting differences between Nigeria and Bolivia. Most of the people groups in Bolivia with which our mission worked numbered only a few hundred or a few thousand. Most language groups in Nigeria are made up of many thousands of people—some, even millions. The Jibu, with 30,000 people, is the smallest with which NBTT worked. In Bolivia, the people considered the missionary to be responsible for the work, at least in the beginning. In Nigeria, every effort was made to help the people see the work as theirs; we were only helpers and advisors. I liked it that way!

Sometimes Anne used to handle hundreds of medical cases a month in Bolivia. In Nigeria, it would have been unwise, probably even illegal, for her to do medical work.

In Bolivia, Spanish is the national language, and except for the indigenous people, Spanish is the first language and mother tongue of the people. There is a great emotional attachment to Spanish and for 200 years it has served as a unifying factor in the nation. In Nigeria, English is the national language, but there is not the same emotional attachment and love for English, as nearly everybody speaks one of the 400 languages as his heart language. Also, many speak Hausa or some other trade language, so English is a distant "third" in many cases. It is therefore amazing that, with few factors of language and culture to unify it, the country has held together during the nearly 50 years of its independence.

In the lowlands of Bolivia, most farmers and hunters carry their guns wherever they go, hoping to come upon meat for the family. In the Jibu region of Nigeria firearms are discouraged; hunters use spears and seem to do well with them in the dry season when the grasslands are being burned off.

Very few of the Jibu even know their age or birthday, as this is not an important item in their culture. This is in contrast to Bolivia where everybody likes to have a big birthday feast of chicken, pork, or beef for family and friends.

Our village house in Nigeria, especially with the solar energy system for lights and with the kerosene refrigerator, was a notch or two superior to what we had when we were with the Sirionó in Bolivia.

In Memory of Mama

Lorna Newell Priest
Nov. 17, 1905 - May 28, 1997

"Thank you, Father, for giving me as a mother one of your dearest. You must have known how much I would need her, and how long."

Mama put her trust in Jesus at an early age, and her devotion to Him was a testimony to all who knew her.

She knew how to "make memories" that for me would last a lifetime. One of my first memories is of her and Daddy sitting under the pear tree with me, both of them laughing and feeding me bits of ripe pear. Another early memory is of her showing me pictures of Christ on the cross, and explaining the meaning.

Mama taught school for three years before I was born, then stayed at home for 18 years, until Dan, Sid, then Janet were of school age. (She did teach for Daddy every year during the World Series, when he'd sit by the radio with score pad on his knee, recording every detail of the games!)

Her hands were never idle. She made sore knees well, drew buckets and buckets of water from the well, washed clothes by hand, made underclothes for us from fertilizer sacks and shirts from colored feed sacks, helped pay for groceries with hens and eggs, helped us milk 18 cows, chopped cotton, cured our meat, kept delicious meals on the table for a growing family, and made the best fruit cobblers and 'nana puddin' this side of heaven.

And how unselfish! I think I was almost grown before I realized that the gizzard, neck, and back weren't really her favorite pieces of chicken.

As a child I thought Mama was the prettiest person in the world, and I loved her long black hair. Right after we got electricity, her hair got caught in the fan, and part of it had to be cut off. It was a sad day for all of us.

Each time I'd go astray, she seemed to know how to help me learn the right lesson. When I was about 10, my friend Donnie offered me a nickel to do something I wasn't supposed to do. I agreed, thinking of that wonderful PAYDAY candy bar I could get with the bribe money. That night Mama showed me a nickel and said, "Donnie left this for you. He said you'd know what it was for." I denied all knowledge, so she said, "I'll give it to you when you tell me the truth." That day I felt I had sold my soul and my integrity (and I didn't even get the PAYDAY!). But I learned my first lesson on how one sin leads to others—first disobedience, then lies, cover-up, and blaming others. Much later, maybe 20 or 30 years later, when I told her all the facts, she went to her purse, handed me the nickel, and said, "Now you can have it."

Mama was faithful to her Methodist church, and in later years usually went to the Baptist as well, since services were in the same building, but they were at different hours. Even when her hearing failed, she'd say, "Church and Sunday School are where I want to be on Sunday."

She instilled acceptance of others in her children. She truly believed that "red and yellow, black and white, all are precious in His sight." She never called a person by a nickname like Fatty, Lard, Slim, or Shorty. Never once did she use a derogatory name for someone of another race, even when "everyone else" was doing it. She believed every individual, every race, deserved the dignity of being called what they preferred to be called.

Sixty years ago when black crippled Annie would come to visit Mama, Daddy would sometimes offer to drive her home in the late afternoon, but she'd have some excuse as to why she should spend the night. She and Mama were friends.

One day around 1940 Mama sat me down at the table to eat with my black friend Mose. I knew it was not a mistake. She was teaching me something even then.

A man in Nigeria once said to me, "We've heard lots about racial tensions, injustices, and attitudes in the Deep South USA. How is it you are able to come here, live and fellowship with blacks and seem to enjoy it?" My answer: "My Mama."

Mama loved our spouses (Anne, Glenda, Imogene, and Neal) as much as she loved her children. When I married she told me, wisely I believe, that if Anne and I should have a dispute, she would take up for Anne.

When our four children came from Bolivia to attend high school and college, they spent many vacations and summers with Daddy and Mama. Once when our boys did something sort of outlandish, I teased Mama by saying, "You didn't bring up our kids very well." Her answer: "I did the best I could with the raw material you gave me." She always had a good sense of humor.

It was difficult for Mama to see me, then me and my family, leave for the mission field, but she was always supportive. After we had been in Bolivia for some years she told me the story of how

I almost died at age three. At that point, Mama committed me to God, then told Him if He spared me, she was giving me to Him for full-time Christian service. So she wasn't at all surprised when I told the family as a teenager that I had felt God's call.

Mama, this is not goodbye. I know you are now with Jesus in heaven, where His nail-scarred hands may be the only reminder of our sins. I'll join you there soon, not because of any good thing I've ever done, but because Jesus died for me. "Nothing in my hand I bring, only to thy cross I cling."

Attributes of God

Wherever I've gone—Bolivia, Mexico, Peru, Brazil, Nigeria, Kenya, Ghana—I've noticed that the local people cook over an open fire, usually outside, and the cooking pot rests on three stones. Why not just two? There would be no supper; the pot could not balance properly. Why not four? One would be useless as the pot rests best on three.

I see the three stones as representing the three all-inclusive attributes of God: love, power, and wisdom.

God's grace, mercy, and loving-kindness can be considered as manifestations of his *love*.

His creation and control of the universe, His working in the hearts of people, and His miracles are manifestations of His *power*.

His Word, His plan for our salvation and spiritual growth, His knowledge, His insight, and His ability to discern our innermost thoughts are the results of His *wisdom*.

It is impossible that His love, His power, or His wisdom would ever diminish. But just imagine what would happen if God should lose one of these attributes.

A God of love and power, but without wisdom, would be a God who wanted to do the best for us, but bungle it up, every time, badly.

A God of love and wisdom, but without power, would plan wisely for our good, but He would be a weakling, unable to make it happen.

A God of power and wisdom, but without love, would be a hideous ogre.

When I see the three-stone fireplaces, I thank God that He is a God of love, power, and wisdom—just what I need Him to be for me.

Keeping On

Wars, depressions, and terrorism have been some of the horrors in our lifetimes. But we have also witnessed other, more encouraging developments, and have benefited from inventions more positive and useful than high-tech weaponry, for example medical advances and missionary aviation. Our language tasks have become more manageable and more accurate as we've enlarged our "tool kit" to include inventions such as the tape recorder, electric typewriter, white-out, photocopiers, computers, and compact disc.

Even more exciting has been the privilege of knowing and working together with devoted brothers and sisters of many nationalities in the work of Bible translation and related tasks. We helped train dozens of Africans, and some are persevering in the task against almost insurmountable odds.

We will always be thankful to the Lord for taking us to Bolivia and then to Nigeria and for the ministry he gave us in those countries. We love the Sirionó and Jibu peoples and long to see them turn to Christ in greater numbers and greater commitment.

We left Nigeria when we had a combined age of 136 years, and we agreed with the WBT administration that it was time to take a "reduced assignment" in the USA for a year or two before retirement. We were ready to move on to whatever the Lord had for us in the next stage of life. Anne and I were appointed by Wycliffe as representatives for the state of South Carolina to promote Bible translation and missions in Christian and secular colleges, in churches, and among individuals. Our desire is to help Christians of all ages be involved in the very thing that God has told the Church to do: evangelize the world for Jesus. We are convinced that every believer should be involved in some vital way in missions, and we want as many as possible not to miss out on the opportunity. We enjoy talking to young people about ministry to those still waiting to hear about the Lord. For the past eight years we have taught an hispanic Sunday School class (Bible and English). Ladies from many churches attend a large weekly women's Bible study class that Anne teaches at Temple Baptist Church. Just recently one young man, whom we didn't remember ever having seen, told us he is now a Wycliffe missionary partly because of our influence. Things like that, plus God's wonderful grace, keep us going.

Glossary

- **Ambaibo**—tree in Bolivia. The English name is Cecropia.
- **Bato**—one of the largest storks in the Americas. The English name is Jabiru.
- **Cabeza seca**—large stork. The English name is Wood Stork.
- **Capybara**—largest rodent in the world. It can weigh over 100 pounds.
- **Children's Home**—school dormitory for the missionary children
- **Cochabamba**—city in the Bolivian highlands where many went for medical needs, work, vacations, and shopping
- **Eoco**—Sirionó name for Perry, meaning "Tall-one"
- **Estados Unidos**—the United States
- **Ibiato**— second Sirionó village where we lived. Other spellings include Eviato and Ebiato
- **Jos**—NBTT headquarters in Nigeria
- **Micro**—bus which accepts as many passengers as can squeeze inside and sometimes hanging outside
- **Novia**—Spanish word for girlfriend
- **NBTT**—Nigeria Bible Translation Trust, under whom we worked in Nigeria
- **Normal School**—school for training teachers
- **Patron**—Spanish word for guardian, protector, owner
- **Riberalta**—town nearest to Tumi Chucua where there were some medical facilities
- **San Pedro**—first Sirionó village we lived in. A ranch run by don Abram Richards with the Sirionó as his workers.
- **Señora**—Spanish word for married woman, the Sirionó sometimes called Anne Señora
- **Serti**—town in Nigeria where we lived
- **Shin**—guinea corn beer
- **SIM/ECWA**—a sister mission
- **Tacana**—one of the indigenous groups of Bolivia
- **Tumi Chucua**—our center of operations in Bolivia
- **WBT**—Wycliffe Bible Translators
- **Yuca**—cassava or manioc

Made in the USA
Columbia, SC
13 August 2020

16157113R00070